Hang Tough!

Life in the public eye: Gov. Grant Sawyer dances the "twist" with Evelyn Roen at a benefit in 1962. This photograph was widely reproduced, and it appeared in the Soviet newspaper, *Izvestia*, as an illustration of American "moral decay."

Hang Tough!

grant sawyer: an activist
in the governor's mansion

university of nevada
oral history program

from oral history interviews
with grant sawyer,
conducted by gary e. elliott,
a narrative composed by r.t. king

Publication of *Hang Tough!* was made possible in part
by a generous contribution from the firm of
Lionel Sawyer & Collins. Additional funds
were provided by Mary-Ellen and Sam McMullen,
and by Robert L. McDonald.

University of Nevada Oral History Program
Reno, Nevada 89557

Library of Congress Cataloging in Publication Data:

Sawyer, Grant, 1918-
Hang tough! grant sawyer: an activist in the governor's mansion :
from oral history interviews with Grant Sawyer /
conducted by Gary E. Elliott; a narrative composed by R.T. King.
p.   cm.
Includes index.
ISBN 1-56475-367-0
1. Sawyer, Grant, 1918-   .   2. Governors—Nevada
—Biography.   3. Nevada—Politics and government.   I. Elliott,
Gary E., 1941-   .   II. King, R.T. (Robert Thomas), 1944-   .   III.
Title.
F845.25.S29A3   1993
979.3'033'092--dc20
[B]   93-30102
CIP

Publication Staff:
production manager Helen M. Blue
senior production assistant Linda J. Sommer
production assistants Verne W. Foster, Amy R. Thomson

Contents

Preface

H ANG TOUGH! is my fifth narrative interpretation of an oral history. For each I have written prefatory remarks discussing the procedures which shaped the work. Since this preface will differ from the others only in detail, readers who are already familiar with what I have to say about oral history interviewing and narrative composition may wish to go directly to Grant Sawyer's story. However, those who have no acquaintance with the methods of the University of Nevada Oral History Program (UNOHP) are encouraged to stick with me. Although there is nothing exciting here — no revelations of secretly-recorded conversations or mysterious tape erasures — I do try to explain the book's derivation, its organization, and the structure of its language, all of which depart in significant (but I hope not disturbing) ways from the traditional format of published memoir.

Unlike memoir, oral history is the product of a collaboration, its content and form significantly influenced by the questions of an interviewer. For our interviewer on this project we were fortunate to have Gary E. Elliott, a member of the faculty of Southern Nevada Community College who is emerging as an authority on the history of government and politics in Nevada, and whose book, *Senator Alan Bible and the Making of the New American West*, will be published by the University of Nevada Press in the spring of 1994. Dr. Elliott gained valuable interviewing experience while researching the career of Senator Bible; and before beginning the Sawyer project he met with me for additional training, and I asked him to do some reading in oral history theory and method. When the time came to commence the interviewing, we were in close agreement on how to proceed.

Recognizing that Gov. Sawyer and Dr. Elliott would be engaged in an "imaginative reconstruction of the past" (to use R. G. Collingwood's apt description of history in general), we sought to bring Sawyer's memories to the surface in a net of proven historiographic weave, which, carefully cast, can capture essential form and substance that are generally absent from unguided reminiscences. While preparing for the interviews, Elliott had access to Gov. Sawyer's private papers.[1] Using these and other sources, we put together a matrix of subjects and chronology, and Elliott developed a detailed but flexible plan for the work. As the months of interviewing and review unfolded, he occasionally found himself following Gov. Sawyer into unexpected terrain, but whether leading or following, he always conducted the interviews in such a way that the governor was prompted to reveal change over time, causality, and sequential development (one thing leading to another) where they had occurred. Governor Sawyer was also encouraged to provide specific examples in support of generalities, and to be analytical and reflective about his life, his career, and the actions of the many public figures he had encountered in its course.

During a nine-month period in 1991, Dr. Elliott and Gov. Sawyer recorded thirty-two tapes from which UNOHP staff eventually produced a transcript over twelve hundred pages long. This transcript was not easy to read and understand; in fact, it was a trial. Only in the particular, only within each discrete part was there any apparent coherence. And the voices of Sawyer and Elliott, two men who in real life are impressively articulate, were often almost unintelligible. In short, we had a typical verbatim transcript. Oral discourse can be practically impenetrable when represented in print: empty of gesture, inflection, tone, and other nuances that go unrecorded on tape, or for which there are no symbols on the keyboard, transcripts are full of fractured syntax, false starts, repetition, and general disorder. Scholars willing to accept the challenge of reading transcripts often find them to be filled with information, but the form will never reach a wide audience.

Hang Tough! is an effort to make the fruits of oral history methodology coherent and accessible. Composed to read as a first-person account by Grant Sawyer, it is my narrative treatment of the record that Sawyer and Elliott created. (Although the verbatim transcript of their interviews is five times longer than the book, nothing of substance in the former is missing from the latter.) Throughout, I have interpreted Sawyer's speech as faithfully as possible consistent with the aim of composing a narrative from the elements of the interviews, but the reader is advised that these are rarely Sawyer's words precisely as spoken. Furthermore, Dr. Elliott's questions, which established the structure and elicited the detail of the work, have been subsumed into the narrative, and I have imposed a measure of chronological and topical order on the text that was not always evident in the transcript. (In this I had valuable assistance from Helen Blue, who did the first rough reorganization of the material.)

While I wished to compose a readable narrative, I would not permit form to dictate content. As a consequence, the book's organization is a compromise. (This is particularly apparent in Part Three.) Throughout the work oral history's natural episodic structure is reflected by occasional abrupt transitions from subject to subject. These leaps are indicated in the text by a break between paragraphs. The reader will also encounter at least two departures from conventional composition: when Gov. Sawyer laughs in amusement or to express irony, I represent this with [laughter]; and ellipses are used not to indicate that material has been deleted, but that a statement has been interrupted or is incomplete . . . or there is a pause for dramatic effect.

Grant Sawyer has read the finished manuscript in page proof form, and affirms that it accurately interprets the content of the interviews from which it is drawn. Still, I hope that there will be readers who are interested in the unaltered record: copies of the tape recordings of the interviews are in the archives of the Oral History Program of the University of Nevada, Reno, where they can be heard by appointment. As with all our oral histories, while we can vouch for the authenticity and general accuracy of *Hang Tough!* the UNOHP does not claim that the work is entirely free of error. Intelligent readers will approach it with the same anticipation of discovery, tempered with caution, that they would bring to government records, newspaper accounts, diaries, memoirs, and other sources of historical information.

ROBERT THOMAS KING
University of Nevada, Reno

Acknowledgments

No oral history project of this magnitude would be possible without help. The UNOHP is indebted to many people, chief among whom is Grant Sawyer, who didn't have to go along with a proposal that would absorb hundreds of hours of his time and cause him considerable anxiety over a period of two and a half years. Conscientious in his preparation for the interviews, and direct in his answers, Gov. Sawyer endured the whole thing with great good humor. We hope he is as happy with the outcome as we are.

Work such as this requires external funding. Through generous supporting grants to the UNOHP, the law firm of Lionel Sawyer & Collins was instrumental in the success of this project. Additional gifts from Mary-Ellen and Sam

McMullen, and from Robert L. McDonald, helped defray the considerable expense of publication. For all of this, we are deeply appreciative. We recognize that in a very real sense the support from our benefactors is a gift to the reading public of Nevada.

At every stage of the project we had the enthusiastic and capable assistance of a number of individuals and institutions. Anthony N. Cabot, a scholar in lawyer's clothing, was influential in securing Grant Sawyer's participation, and he gave lasting impetus to the work. The bright, cheerful, and extraordinarily efficient Rosemary Congero, Gov. Sawyer's personal secretary, contributed mightily to our success. In no particular order, we are also indebted to the following for their help and their commitment to enriching Nevada's historical record: Guy Rocha and Jeff Kintop of the Nevada State Archives; Don Dondero; Prof. Elmer Rusco; Duncan Aldrich, Joanne Guyton, Alisa Huckle, Sharon Prengaman, Mike Simons and Kathryn Totton of the UNR Library; David Millman, Nevada State Museum and Historical Society, Las Vegas; Susan Jarvis and Dennis McBride, Special Collections, UNLV Library; Lee Mortensen, Eric Moody and Nita Phillips, Nevada Historical Society, Reno; Dennis Myers, KTVN TV; Gerald Edwards and Larry Dobbs, Colorado River Commission; Joanie Hammack, Nevada Gaming Control Board; the staff of the Churchill County Museum; Shawn Hall, Northeastern Nevada Museum; Ed Kelly; Thomas Mitchell, *Las Vegas Review-Journal*; and Kathy O'Connell, Cal-Neva Lodge. Finally, and as always, we are thankful to Tom Radko, Nick Cady, Cam Sutherland and the staff of the University of Nevada Press for their expert technical advice.

Introduction

Several years ago, a friend of mine asked me what classes I was teaching. When I replied Nevada history, he chuckled and said: "Nevada doesn't have a history." At the time I thought little about that casual remark, but I have given it considerable thought in the last couple of years. As someone who has taught, researched, and published in the field of Nevada history, I have come to the conclusion that, like my friend, the impression most people have of Nevada is limited to Las Vegas's Strip and Glitter Gulch (Fremont Street in downtown Las Vegas). I am also convinced that Nevada's image is persistently and overwhelmingly negative because of the perception that the state is controlled by mobsters. Such widely held notions are reinforced by popular films like *The Godfather* and books such as *The Green Felt Jungle.* Add to this list easy divorce, prostitution, and a scandal-ridden college basketball program, and there exists an indelible imprint that Nevada is someplace to travel though, possibly visit, but certainly no place for respectable people to live.

Governor Grant Sawyer understands the perception of sinful Nevada far better than most because, even as governor, he was often treated (to use his words) "like I had just stepped out from behind some crap table." Governor Sawyer's conflicts with the federal government, particularly J. Edgar Hoover, were in part based on the widespread feeling in Washington, D.C., that Nevada and its people were a rotten lot. Governor Sawyer believes that Nevada's negative image persists and has influenced public policy decisions that have adversely affected the state.

Nevada's tarnished reputation persisted despite its more enlightened public policy positions, and Sawyer played a large role in those. Sawyer began his administration in 1959 with a reorganization program designed to streamline services and increase government efficiency. Nevada was among the leaders in government reform to keep pace with the public's demand for increased services. But government restructuring, no matter how vital, is not among the issues that ignite passions and enlist legions of followers. In short, such policies usually go unnoticed outside the narrow confines of elite discussion groups and political scientists interested in the process of governance. Likewise, gaming control was largely ignored outside of Nevada.

Governor Sawyer was acutely aware that after the Kefauver crime hearings in 1950, Nevada would be judged by how it controlled casino gaming and the people involved in Nevada's "peculiar institution." Consequently, he moved early in his administration to claim the high ground in gaming control though the creation of a new Gaming Control Board.

The board soon established a unique enforcement mechanism officially known as the *List of Excluded Persons*, but unofficially called the "black book." It was a bold move because of its questionable constitutionality. The board was authorized to take action against casino licensees who hosted any person listed in the book. Later, when the constitutionality of the black book was upheld by state and federal courts, much to Sawyer's surprise, it became a fixture in Nevada's enforcement arsenal. Still, Sawyer's gaming control policy was unpopular with the industry, the state legislature, and Roger Foley, Nevada's attorney general. Sawyer's persistence created many enemies among the gaming elite, but Sawyer remained steadfast in his support of the gaming agents. Despite Sawyer's dogged determination to present an honest enforcement image, however, federal authorities remained skeptical.

Similarly, in 1959, Sawyer charted a new course to change the direction of civil rights in Nevada. In his first message to the legislature, he proposed a civil rights bill to guarantee equal access to public accommodations. However, the plan was dead on arrival because of the opposition of gaming interests who believed that white patrons would not associate with black customers. The power and influence of the gaming industry successfully blocked all meaningful civil rights legislation until 1965, when the state was forced to follow the lead of Congress, which in 1964 had passed the most comprehensive civil rights act since reconstruction.

Between 1959 and 1965, Governor Sawyer used his power and influence to push the cause of civil rights. It was the most salient issue of his administration. When he had the clear legal authority to act, he was decisive. He banned discrimination in all phases of state employment and required state contractors to do the same. When it came to the gaming industry, he tried moral persuasion, and, when that failed, he tried to use his power over licensing to force equal access to public accommodations. But two attorneys general concluded that the governor had no authority to deny a gaming license based on segregation practices. Afterward, he supported civil rights groups that kept the pressure on casino owners to desegregate their facilities.

What is instructive about Sawyer's concern over gaming control, government reorganization, and civil rights, is that Nevada was far more progressive than it is often given credit for being. Despite the state's image and reputation, Sawyer presided over an activist government, and nowhere was that more evident than in the area of civil rights. He was not following a national trend, nor was he supporting a policy position advocated by his friend, John F. Kennedy, who, compared to Sawyer, only embraced the cause of civil rights late in his presidency. When President Kennedy was placating the southern wing of the Democratic party, Sawyer was leading a frontal assault against the most entrenched social and economic interests in Nevada. Sawyer's progressivism was rooted deep in his childhood training. His mother instilled in him a belief in the Democratic party, Franklin D. Roosevelt, and the cause of equal rights. Despite his later pragmatism, and the sense of compromise required of any successful politician, Sawyer never forgot the notion of justice that he inherited from his mother. His dedication to the cause of civil rights and equal justice is the single largest contribution of his administration and his forgotten legacy to post-World War II Nevada.

Still, Sawyer was in many respects typical of most western governors, particularly those in the inter-mountain region. He deplored the federal government's ownership of western lands. He complained often and bitterly, to anyone who would listen, that the western states, not the federal government, should control the land within their borders. However, he never complained about the flood of government dollars in the form of subsidies for his ranching constituents. Grazing fees were kept ridiculously low, and Sawyer objected only when the government proposed an increase. Likewise, he did not complain about government-subsidized water programs like the Newlands Project, the Washoe Project, and the Southern Nevada Water Project, all of which stimulated economic development in Nevada. Predictably, in 1964, Sawyer endorsed the western water plan (Sierra-Cascade Project) to bring Columbia River water to the southwest at an enormous cost to the taxpayer and incalculable damage to the environment. While it may have been good politics to support the plan, it would have been a terrible waste of public resources. Like so many others in the Mountain West, Sawyer's view of federalism seemed limited to a desire for dollars without federal control.

As the election of 1962 approached, Nevada voters had a chance to ratify Sawyer's progressive administration, but his challenger, Lt. Governor Rex Bell, an actor-turned-politician, died shortly after the campaign began. The Republican burden then fell on less widely known Las Vegas Mayor Oran Gragson to represent the GOP. While there was little doubt as to the outcome, 1962 was an important year in the political life of Nevada because Paul Laxalt was elected lieutenant governor, which propelled him into the role of the leading Republican figure in the state.

From the beginning, Sawyer did not trust Laxalt. Their private conversations often turned into news conferences called by Laxalt to attack the governor's policies. Besides being political rivals, Sawyer and Laxalt had little in common in their approach to public policy. Laxalt saw Sawyer's government reorganization plan as a scheme to expel entrenched Republicans from their jobs. (Ironically, eighteen years later Laxalt applauded President Reagan for removing Democrats from the Washington bureaucracy.) He also opposed Sawyer's gaming control practices as too strict. Moreover, between 1962 and 1964, Laxalt was hostile toward civil rights legislation in Nevada and did not change his position until 1964, when Congress passed the national Civil Rights Act. In short, Laxalt represented the status quo, while Sawyer advocated a more progressive social agenda.

The prospect of these two attractive candidates battling each other was all the press could ask for. But in 1964, Laxalt chose to challenge incumbent Democratic Senator Howard Cannon, and lost in the closest election in Nevada history — eighty-four votes. Predictably, as 1966 approached, Laxalt declared his intention to retire Sawyer from the governor's office. He had every reason to be optimistic. He led a well-financed and united party. Coupled with his personal popularity, Laxalt presented a formidable challenge to the two-term incumbent, who had antagonized most of Nevada's economic interests.

Sawyer's position could not have been worse. The Democratic party was divided, and the primary was a divisive affair filled with charges and counter-charges, while the majority of gaming interests opposed Sawyer's reelection. Also, he was running against a third-term tradition which Laxalt skillfully turned to his own advantage. Other factors contributed to Sawyer's defeat, primarily a business recession that resulted in unusually high unemployment in Clark County. But Sawyer was probably correct when he said that with each passing day a governor makes more enemies than friends. After eight years in office, the accumulated enemies outnumbered the lasting friends.

The press dubbed the Laxalt-Sawyer contest "the battle of the century." While the campaign was spirited, it was not mean. Issues were presented and debated with all the usual claims of distortion by each side, but it was remarkably free of personal animosity. Today, Gov. Sawyer believes that

Laxalt's victory was a tremendous favor. He has not run for public office since, even though he has had many opportunities to do so (especially when Democrat Alan Bible retired from the United States Senate in 1974). Clearly, after 1966, Sawyer charted a new and successful career in law. He never looked back and has few regrets.

The most striking personal characteristic about Gov. Sawyer is his sense of humor, which is shown throughout this work. While he can speak long and passionately on issues, when it comes to himself, he is not at all that serious. He can laugh at himself, some of his past political positions, and most of all at the political game of getting elected to office. He speaks candidly about himself, his family, and other prominent politicians, past and present. His only regret is that his daughter Gail was forced to live in the political fish bowl and grow up amidst the swirl of political life. She never had the luxury of being just a little girl.

When Sawyer retired from political office, he did not retire from politics — oh, no. He was the Democratic national committeeman for Nevada from 1968 to 1988, and has been active in party affairs both in Nevada and on the national scene. Since 1985, he has been chairman of the Nevada Commission on Nuclear Projects, which assesses the role of the federal government in sponsoring a nuclear waste depository in Nevada for the benefit of private utility interests. In addition, he has remained active in the cause of civil rights and is a member of the national advisory council of the American Civil Liberties Union and a long-time supporter of the NAACP. The issues that were important to him in 1958 still occupy his time and interest today.

Following consultation with Tom King, the director of the Oral History Program, my approach to the interviews with Gov. Sawyer was first to establish a lasting record of political life and then to place the major events, and issues, into historical perspective. In doing so, I had complete access to Gov. Sawyer's personal papers, campaign literature, tapes, newspaper clippings, financial documents, and much more. I would begin by reading the material mentioned above and, combined with other research, make an outline of the areas to be covered during the interview. Sometimes there was a long list of specific questions and at other times general categories to be discussed. The governor was given the outline a week or so before the interview and we would go over it together before the actual interview began. The result was thirty-two hours of taped conversations producing over twelve hundred pages of transcript. This project would not have been possible without the full cooperation of Gov. Sawyer. At times the experience was painful and serious, while on other occasions, I think he clearly enjoyed himself. Working with him was a pleasure, and I believe we have established a lasting friendship — at least I would like to think so.

GARY E. ELLIOTT
Community College of Southern Nevada

Part One

learning the ropes

1

the political gene

With an occasional pause for an event like the Second World War, I was always running for something — from student election campaigns in junior high school through my unsuccessful try for a third term as Nevada's governor. And even though I have sought no elected office in the succeeding years, I am still an active participant in public life. This desire to be involved in trying to improve conditions and to protect the rights of citizens may be partially ego-driven, but it seems to me to be more a natural, reflexive thing than a self-conscious calculation. My attitudes about civic responsibility and the public's need to guard against the abuse of governmental power probably arise from the unusual circumstances that shaped my early life, and from the passion for politics that may have been the only thing my mother and father had in common. If there is a political gene, I carry it.

M_y paternal grandfather emigrated to New York City from England in the 1870s, married a lady of Scottish ancestry, and started a family. My father, Harry William, was born in 1880, and a few years after his birth the family was broken when Grandfather Sawyer died in an agricultural accident, leaving my father and his sister to be raised by their widowed mother. In his early teens my father ran off with a circus, and he later joined the navy and served in the Spanish-American War on a ship stationed off China. There's no telling what adventures he had after his discharge, but he eventually wound up enrolled in an osteopathic school in Kirksville, Missouri . . . some way or another he finagled his way in. [laughter] While there he met and married my mother, Bula Belle Cameron, a fellow student who was a few years younger than he. Mother was from Wahpeton, North Dakota, the second oldest child in a family of three girls and one boy. Whereas her two sisters were very pretty, my mother wasn't; but she was talented, had an extensive vocabulary, and was sort of a renegade in that she did a lot of things that her older sister, Iola, would not. Grandfather Cameron was a teacher, so there was no question that his children would be educated, and they all went on to college, my mother choosing to study osteopathy.

Following marriage and graduation from osteopathic school, my mother and father moved to Twin Falls, Idaho, where they practiced together as osteopaths for six or seven years before my father was charged with the crime of practicing medicine without a license. Osteopaths were legally confined to a relatively narrow field of practice, and he had strayed from it and done some surgery — it was minor surgery, but he wasn't permitted to do any surgery at all. Dad defended himself against this criminal charge, but was convicted; when he appealed the decision to the supreme court of Idaho, he again argued his own case, and again he lost! Still, I am sure that he did well — he was articulate, he was an excellent speaker with a gorgeous voice, and he had a lot of pizazz . . . and he was very self-confident. (The laws under which Dad was convicted have since been changed, giving osteopaths much more freedom to practice what we now call medicine than they had in those days, but *Idaho* v. *Sawyer* was a landmark case, and it is still cited with respect to the depth of practice that an osteopath can engage in.)

Losing his appeal made my father so mad that he left the family for a summer and went back to some marginal medical school in Kansas City for a short time. The school was little more than a diploma mill, but after Dad got his fly-by-night M.D. certificate and came back to Twin Falls, he spent the rest of his life fighting the osteopaths because they didn't have "real" medical degrees. [laughter] He later went on to build a successful medical practice in Fallon, Nevada, and he eventually wound up as president of the Nevada State Medical Association, which is quite a laugh, considering his osteopathic beginnings. Dad accomplished a lot in his life, and given what I know of his background, it had to be just pure guts and intelligence and drive that got him where he was. In his world, he was extraordinarily successful, even though he would be looked on today as just a simple country doctor from Fallon.

I was born in Twin Falls on December 14, 1918, the youngest of three boys. Our parents divorced when I was three years old, and it was a very messy affair. My only recollection of it is that as my father left the house after the last big fight, I went up and kicked him in the leg! [laughter] There followed episodes of our going into court, with my aunt and grandmother on my father's side trying to get custody of us children, and our teachers being called in to testify at these hearings . . . and Mother was constantly suing Dad for back alimony — that went on for years. Later I learned a lot of things about my parents' relationship, and I came to wonder how they had stayed together as long as they had. They were competing in their professional practices in the same office, and there were accusations of stealing patients from one another (my mother was very aggressive, as was my father), but their domestic problems were even more severe. Apparently it was just an impossible relationship.

Following the divorce my father met Byrd Fanita Wall, one of the daughters of a prominent Twin Falls family. Not too long after that he moved to Nevada, and Byrd followed him, and they were married. Through summer visits we boys gradually got to know my father, and he turned out to be not quite the bogeyman that I had been led to believe . . . and Byrd was just a glorious person. But it really took a few years for us to get to know them and for them to get to know us, because we carried our mother's interpretation of this relation-ship, and we had heard a lot of horror stories about Byrd before we ever met her: "Byrd was the interloper; she was the one who dispossessed our mother." My eldest brother is Harry William, Jr., known as Pete to family and friends, and the second born was Milo Cameron — Milo was extremely partisan toward our mother all of his life (he had difficulty adjusting to the relationship between our father and Byrd), while Pete was closer to our father, and he sort of took Father's side. I was right in the middle, and I didn't believe anything anybody told me! [laughter]

Harry William Sawyer

"My father was a proud man, and quite guarded, and I find myself to be somewhat the same way."

Byrd Wall Sawyer
"As I got to know her, I came to adore her. She was just marvelous!"

By nature Byrd was reserved, a real lady. Although it was difficult for her during the summers that we spent in Fallon, she was terrific and she gave us a lot of things that my mother didn't, because she had a very different personality. For example, my mother would let dirty dishes lie: "They'll still be there tomorrow." She was not the world's greatest housekeeper. As far as Mother was concerned, "Let's get on with the big things, because these other things are mundane and irrelevant." Byrd was quite different. She was precise. If you were supposed to be someplace, you'd be there on time; and if you were supposed to do something, you did it, and you did it right. Byrd was also quite intellectual, so you had to be a good student. My mother didn't care whether you were a good student or not, as long as you got by and moved on. [laughter] Since Byrd did things differently, we were initially very uncomfortable around her. We thought she was real picky about things, and we didn't understand all this stress on eating properly, using the right spoon and that sort of thing. Then as the years went by and I got to know her, I came to adore her. She was just marvelous! She put a quality in my life that I wasn't used to — you had to be proper, you had to be dressed right, you had to have the right manners, you had to send thank-you notes . . . and my mother could have cared less about any of those things. [laughter]

My relationship with my father also warmed up over the years, although it had never been hostile, really — it was just a matter of us getting to know one another. Seeing him only during summers meant that it took several years for us to establish any kind of a relationship. When I was in college, I saw more of Dad because he lived in Fallon and I was in Reno, but it took some years for that relationship to mature, simply because we didn't know one another and we hadn't been close at all during my youth. The divorce and the accusations and turmoil which followed were a source of discomfort to my father, who was a good deal more sensitive than he would let anyone know — he was a proud man and quite guarded, and I find myself to be somewhat the same way. Although I think he felt close to us boys, and was proud of us, it was difficult for him to say so, and we always had to be a little careful about what we said to him. But we were proud of our dad, who had been elected to the Nevada legislature by the time I graduated from high school. To his everlasting credit he never criticized my mother to us, which certainly was not true on her side. He would ask about her once in a while, but he would never ask any of us brothers directly — he'd ask our wives.

Two or three years after my mother and father were divorced, Mother gave up practicing osteopathy and married Ephraim Jones Malone, a farmer who was a deacon in the Twin Falls Baptist church. Mr. Malone's farm was one of forty acres in a little town named Maroa, right out of Filer, Idaho, about fifteen miles from Twin Falls. A couple of years after the marriage, when I was in the third grade, he sold the first farm and bought one much closer to Twin Falls — this one made up of forty acres adjacent to the house, with another forty across the road. Mr. Malone raised hay, beets, and potatoes, and he had the usual cows, pigs and other livestock that all farmers kept in those days . . . and my mother had a vegetable garden, so we were pretty self-sufficient as far as food was concerned.

Mother did the kind of work that all farm wives had to do: she didn't get out and milk the cows or that sort of thing, but she did take care of the household and the cooking and all the other domestic responsibilities such as washing and ironing. During haying time and when the crops came in, the farmers would band together and hire itinerant farm laborers

— people who were out of work and looking for day jobs. Mother would cook for our day laborers, which could number as many as ten or fifteen . . . lunch was the big meal. She cooked over a wood stove for several years before the house was electrified; and even after we got electric power we didn't have inside plumbing for some years, and we used an outhouse. (Eventually we had a live-in housekeeper who helped Mother with everything.)

We boys had chores. Pete, who was ten or twelve when my mother married Mr. Malone, did a lot more than Milo or me (we were pretty young), but we milked the cows and we had other assignments — slopping the pigs and that sort of thing — which we did after we came home from school each day. In the summers we would work out in the fields, haying and with the beets and the potatoes, and we had a potato cellar where we put potatoes to let them sprout for planting the following year. Farm life was pretty bleak, and I didn't care for it at all, but I wasn't really conscious during those years of being deprived of anything. We always had plenty to eat — we would kill the pigs and the cattle, and we grew all our own vegetables, and we had our own milk from which my mother used to make butter.

I attended Washington Grammar School in Twin Falls, and Twin Falls High School, whose enrollment was about five hundred. I was a mediocre student — no genius, I'll tell you that — but in high school I was interested in dramatics and I kept my grades up high enough to be eligible to perform in nearly all of the plays. (You had to have a certain level of grades or you couldn't be involved in extracurricular activities.) Going to school my brothers and I rode the bus, but we often walked home because we did many things that required us to stay after school. This was a cause of deep resentment on the part of Mr. Malone: we should be out there milking the cows, as far as he was concerned, and I think he was also somewhat resentful because we were doing things that his own children had never done, never aspired to do.

When I was a junior in high school, I won the Idaho state oratorical contest, and was eligible to participate in the national declamation finals. The school would pay for the trip, but I didn't own a suit; I didn't have anything to wear. We finally decided that I had to have a jacket of some kind, and this jacket would cost seven dollars. My mother had no income of her own, so Mr. Malone was brought into the picture; but not only did he not have a particularly high income, he was also very tight: he *lent* me the seven dollars. [laughter] After about three hundred times practicing it, I was so panicked when I gave my speech that I forgot it; but I think I wound up fourth, and the winner, to my best recollection, was Orson Welles.

My brothers and I worked every summer at something, the money being saved for our education, and occasionally Mr. Malone would give us a meager sum for working on the farm. Years afterwards, going to class reunions with my schoolmates, they've told me how sorry they used to feel for me because we were so poor. Now, I never felt poor; I never had that feeling at all. But they did, so I guess we were. [laughter] When Mr. Malone and my mother were divorcing and they got into the question of community property, it turned out that there wasn't any to speak of. (I always had some kind of job. When I went to Linfield College, I worked on campus in the summer. After transferring to the University of Nevada I worked for the highway department one summer with my older brother; another summer, I worked in a mine in Nevada — my father happened to be the executor of the estate of which the mine was a part — and earned pretty good wages.)

Mr. Malone's children were older than I was, and I would guess that he was thirty years older than my mother; and even though we lived with him for a number of years, we didn't have much in common with Mr. Malone and his family. He wasn't really interested in the outside world, and he disapproved of us staying after school to rehearse for plays or participate in athletics, and so forth, because he thought all of that stuff was irrelevant, fancy living. Mother sort of served as a barrier between Mr. Malone and us boys, and she handled our upbringing; but occasionally he would attempt to discipline us, and that would cause another fight. Aunt Fern (my mother's younger sister) was a school teacher who lived in Hansen, a small town near Twin Falls, and when there was a family fight we kids would be shipped out to stay with her until it blew over. I was very close to Aunt Fern when I was young, and she exercised a major influence on my development.

Mr. Malone was quite compulsive about his religion, and as a result we spent a lot of time in church, which was OK; nobody objected to it. In fact, I think my mother was a Sunday school teacher at one point. We got drilled in all of these principles, and were admonished to be honest and to be fair, and it later turned out that my stepfather was a cheat: when he took our wheat in to be weighed, he was putting iron bars or something down in it. [laughter] This left quite an impression on me. He presented a pillar-of-the-church facade, but in his business life he was doing just the opposite of what a religious person would do. That may have been the first time in my life that I realized that people aren't always what they seem. Even though I later went to a Baptist college, as a young man I turned away from the institutional church, probably because of what I had seen in Mr. Malone.

My mother and Mr. Malone were totally incompatible. I think she married him only because she was looking for some security for her three boys; it was just that simple. They had very little, if anything, in common, and they were divorced when I was a senior in high school, which would have been

1936. It was a very dirty divorce, with accusations of adultery and just generally seamy . . . . My mother, as usual, was very aggressive, and that divorce went to the supreme court of Idaho. By then I was the only son left at home, and of course I was getting only my mother's side of the story. The divorce left such a bad taste in my mouth that I just wanted to forget it, blank the events out of my mind. And I have, to a large extent.

Although I never cared for Mr. E. J. Malone, in fairness it must be said that during all that turbulent time I was developing a slanted view. In such a situation you usually don't have much regard for your adversary, but in retrospect I understand that he was in a very difficult position, and I am much less critical of him now than I was in those days. Think what it must have been like living with my mother and three of her progeny! His interests were so very different from ours that he probably felt isolated, alone, and inadequate. After leaving Twin Falls I would return from time to time, and I learned a little more and got closer to some of Mr. Malone's children and their families, and I found them to be pretty decent people. It had just been one of those things where everybody was in a difficult situation . . . nobody's fault.

My mother was a Democrat; and, for those days in Idaho, an extremely liberal Democrat with a strong social conscience, always involved in taking care of the poor. (She also belonged to the order of the Eastern Star, in which she eventually wound up the Worthy Grand Matron for the state of Idaho.) Mother was a pretty good speaker and an excellent organizer, and she had a talent for bringing people together and enunciating goals and objectives and getting them done. During the Depression she ran an operation that cooked meals for homeless people, and I remember her passing out pamphlets on the street about various things. I am sure she was considered to be a raving radical — which I guess she was by Idaho standards. [laughter] Mother felt that everyone should have a fair shake and an equal opportunity, no matter who they were or what their circumstances. That was the foundation of her outlook on virtually everything. That's what I lived with all during my youth, and I believe that I owe much of *my* lifelong social sensitivity to being reared in that atmosphere: I give her credit for that. She impressed her social conscience on Milo, too, but she didn't have the same effect on Pete, who has been quite conservative all his life — I am not even sure he is a Democrat! [laughter]

There were few minorities in Twin Falls, and race was not in my consciousness then, but I've since thought about it a lot. The father of the only black family in town was a boot-black who had his stall outside the Perrine Hotel, and he and his wife's two children were in my class, twins. I got to know them quite well and have stayed in touch with them — I've seen them from time to time over the years since then. The family was pretty much accepted by the community, and it didn't seem that they were discriminated against. America may have been wrestling with the issue of race, but we were so isolated in Twin Falls that I didn't even realize there was a problem! I certainly was aware, however, of distinctions based on social class. Twin Falls, with its banks, merchants, and professional people, was the center of a largely agricultural community, and the gulf between the town students and the farm students was great. Town people acted a little superior to the farm kids, and I experienced that attitude firsthand when I got to high school. Some evidence of it can still be seen at class reunions.

Although I was president of my junior high, I was not elected to any office in high school. I had gotten pretty cocky, and when I wasn't even invited to join a high school fraternity until I was a junior, it almost killed me — it was quite a blow to my ego. Today I feel high school fraternities and sororities should be banned, because they are so destructive to the poor girl or boy sitting there hoping somebody will ask them to be in this phony social set-up. I was deeply wounded, and when I have gone to class reunions and seen men who were in a fraternity and wouldn't invite me to join . . . . More than anything in the world I have always wanted people to accept and trust and respect me, and if they wouldn't do so on their terms, I would try to make them do it on mine. But I was rejected in high school. I've thought about that experience a lot, and I believe it may be that I went over the line, which I later learned is a risk in every political setting. You can move so fast, but if you move any faster than that, and particularly if you are not very careful or discreet about how you do it, you arouse a lot of resentment and suddenly find yourself not a hero but an anti-hero: everybody is out to show you that you have stepped over the line. That's what happened to me. I was considered to be a poor farm kid, and the town kids were out to show me my place . . . and they succeeded.

Not being accepted into a fraternity was one of the most traumatic experiences in my life. I carry it with me to this day. It changed my behavior: from it I learned that in dealing with others you can move in the direction that you believe is right, but you have to be very careful about how you do it if you want to accomplish something. You can blow yourself out of the water by getting so far out that you lose respect and acceptance, and you're discarded. Simply because *you* know something is right doesn't mean that everybody is going to agree with you; and arguing the point isn't going to convince them — you have to do it in some other fashion, and you have to be patient and careful. I learned that I couldn't live in

an isolated world and be so cocksure that what I was doing
was the great thing.

In high school, speech
and theater were my primary interests, and I starred in
virtually every play that was performed. My speech teachers
would tell me at the end of each semester, "Your grades next
semester have to be so-and-so if you are to continue to have
roles in plays," and they would be just that. Wilma Keele was
a business teacher, and although I wasn't great in that field I
liked her; and the French teacher was a little thing and very
cute, and I liked her very much and I liked French very
much. [laughter] I was involved in athletics, particularly in
track, but I was no great star; I also played some basketball.
My eyes were very bad, even then, limiting what I could do.
If I played football it would have to be with my glasses on,
and with that big grillwork mask that went over your face . . .
it didn't work too well.

The football coach was also the principal of the school.
One time a teacher accused me of propositioning one of the
girls, and I was called into his office. When my mother found
out, she marched down to the high school, and, much to my
embarrassment, she raised hell with the principal and put
everybody on the mat. I was exonerated. [laughter]

I don't know where she got the money, but my mother got
us all private speech lessons, elocution lessons. (Our teacher
was a lady from the church, and maybe she didn't charge for
the lessons; we never did know.) In addition to taking
elocution lessons, I was also learning how to tap dance, and
Martha Morehouse and I used to tap around the county at
Grange meetings and various other gatherings. When we
finished a performance people would throw money out on
the floor, and we would collect it and split it between us. We

loved to dance together — ballroom dancing, too. I was very
fond of Martha . . . still am. She and her family have been
dear friends of mine since we started dancing. We get
together occasionally when she comes through Las Vegas,
and we still dance when we see each other; she is a great
dancer. (People later kidded me about being a politician and
a tap dancer at the same time. [laughter] When I set up
practice in Elko, fresh out of law school, there was a minstrel
show there, and all the time that we lived in Elko I tap
danced in the show. In fact I tapped right up to the time
when my body began to decay and my left foot wouldn't
work very well anymore.)

With the exception of
one course, my primary/secondary education was pretty
good: I wasn't at all interested in sixth-grade mathematics, and
didn't learn a thing, and I've never been able to add two and
two since that day. My poor daughter is in the same boat, so
maybe it's a matter of genes. [laughter] But there's a total
blank, and how I ever got through later math courses I don't
know, because after failing to learn the basics in the sixth
grade I never understood math; I don't understand it now;
and I don't even know what calculus *means*. When I got to
college, I had to take some math courses, and I barely
managed to bluff my way through.

I had some friendships with high school classmates that
have endured, and I've stayed in distant contact with many of
the people with whom I graduated from high school. I have
also been back to Twin Falls for several class reunions, going
even when I was governor. Old classmates now seem quite
different from the way I remember them in high school . . .
particularly the women. Many girls who were then hot stuff

are now old, fat ladies, and some of the ones we used to call "dogs" in high school became really glamorous women.

My mother and her side of the family were resolved that we brothers would go on for higher education. As poor as we were, there was never any question from the day we were born that we were going to go to college — it wasn't even a subject for debate. Nobody knew how, but we were going to go! Actually, I would have preferred to become an actor, but at high school graduation I didn't have any *specific* objective except to get out into the world and find out what was going on and see what I could do. I certainly had no desire to be a farmer. [laughter] The sooner I could get away from home, the better. (The idea of a career in law only came along later when I recognized that it was economically too risky for me to be standing in Hollywood casting lines and that sort of thing in light of my negatives, which were substantial — I was not good looking, and I was not very impressive physically. I decided that the wise thing would be to try to become a lawyer; then I could do some of the same things I would if I were in the theater, and still be able to make a living. [laughter])

After her divorce from Mr. Malone, my mother and I moved into a little apartment in town. I was working after school and at night in the Safeway store as a boxman, and we faced the problem of whether I could go on to college. Mother was very depressed and despondent, and she exhibited symptoms of what I came to believe was sort of a gradual disintegration of her spirit. She suddenly decided that I shouldn't go to college — I should stay home and take care of her. But that was totally contrary to everything she'd taught us to aspire to all our lives. Well, my aunt Fern and some of my mother's lady friends in town heard about this, and they

came and took me away from that apartment. I remember my
mother pleading and crying, but they just took me down and
put me on the bus to go to Linfield, and that's how I got to
college. I don't know whether I would have had the nerve to
do it myself; I don't suppose I would have. That was the first
sign I saw of some sort of mental problem with my mother,
and as the years went by she got much, much worse.

Because of Mr. Malone's connection with the Baptist
church we brothers were given scholarships to Linfield
College, and through scholarships and working, we were able
to make it without financial assistance from our families. That
was probably the cheapest college education we could get
under the circumstances. Linfield was a small college, and a
very close community. I lived in a dormitory and I joined
Alpha Gamma Nu: I wasn't against fraternities; I was just
against the ones that wouldn't let me in! [laughter] I made
some good friends there, and a couple of years ago we went
to the first reunion I've been to, and I saw nearly all of them.
One year when I was governor I went back to give the
commencement address, which was kind of funny in light of
my experience there — I was sort of a rebel like my dad was,
and Linfield was so strict that I ended up being thrown
out . . . .

My first year there I immediately got involved in campus
politics, and I was elected president of the freshman class;
Milo was president of the sophomore class at the same time.
The next year I was elected to the student council as the
representative of the sophomore class, and Milo was also on
that. But I wound up rocking the boat. Since Linfield was a
Baptist school it was very restrictive regarding social behavior,
and I became restive about what I thought were superficial
rules. The Dean of Women even put out a bulletin that set
down standards of behavior for when there were so many
people in a car that a girl had to sit on the lap of a boy. She

described the kind of pillow that must be inserted between the boy and the girl. [laughter] You couldn't smoke, drink, or do any of the things that everybody else could do. You couldn't even dance! I became rebellious. The president of the college was a retired general, and he ran the place like a military camp, so some other rebels and I got together and threw a dance downtown in mock honor of him — we displayed a big picture of him behind the band that we had hired. We publicized the dance all over campus, and it was a terrific success, but the president called me in and stated that since I couldn't follow the rules, they would have to expel me. I relayed that to my mother, and she came over from Twin Falls and marched in to see him, and they had it out. We finally compromised by my consenting not to come back the following year.

When I left Linfield I transferred to the University of Nevada, because my father lived in Nevada and he could help me a little bit financially. Plus my older brother Pete had gone through the same thing: he wasn't kicked out of Linfield, but after his sophomore year he transferred to Nevada. Going from Linfield to the University of Nevada was like going from one end of the social spectrum to the other, because in those days Nevada was really pretty swinging. Shortly after I got to Reno I went to a fraternity dance and arrived as they were carrying a body out. It turned out to be a faculty advisor; he was drunk, passed out. [laughter] I was amazed at the difference in atmosphere from Linfield, and I was delighted!

In courses that I liked, both at Linfield and Nevada, I did very well; but in courses that I didn't like, I didn't. (I later did much better in law school than I ever did in college because I liked law — I really enjoyed it, and I got very good grades. I had never had a high grade average before, either in high school or in college.) At Nevada I majored in philosophy, and Reuben Thompson, the father of Bruce and Gordon

Thompson, was the head of the department. (Gordon was in my class, and a close friend of mine; he was later a member of the Nevada supreme court.) I worked for Professor Thompson as a paper grader, and I thought that his classes were superb. I thoroughly enjoyed philosophy, and did well in it because I liked it, I guess.

My junior year I pledged Alpha Tau Omega, and the next year I was elected its president. I was also involved in dramatics, was in all the plays, and I was in Coffin and Keys, a very mysterious organization — so mysterious that I never understood what the mystery was. [laughter] (Coffin and Keys was a select group of students, campus leaders who sort of set policy and ran things politically and otherwise at the university, and it is still very much in evidence at Nevada.) A lot of my friends from the university still live in Nevada, and although you don't tend to have relationships as close as you did when you belonged to a fraternity, you see your old friends and you remain brothers. That was particularly evident when I ran for governor. Nearly every community that I went into had some ATOs, whether they were in my class or not, and we had that fraternal feeling, or at least the feeling that we had something in common. Regardless of whether they were Republicans or Democrats, they were out supporting me.

There was a lot to be said for going to college in Nevada if you were going to live in the state, because your classmates would be important to you the rest of your life. This was more true of the university then, and of the Reno campus now, than it is of the University of Nevada-Las Vegas. The UNLV students tend to be more migratory and from out of state, whereas most of the University of Nevada students at that time were from old Nevada families that are still here. My whole experience at the University of Nevada was wonderful, and I remember it with nothing but positive feelings. Relation-

ships that developed while I was there, the whole atmosphere . . . they were two of the best years of my life. I don't
look back at Linfield with that same euphoric feeling, but the
University of Nevada was just terrific!

2

service: mccarran
and the military

My father and Senator Pat McCarran were close friends, and while I was a student at the University of Nevada Dad said to him, "I've got a son who wants to go to law school."

McCarran replied, "I'll take care of it. Send him to me in Washington."

Unfortunately, by the time I graduated they had had a dispute and weren't speaking; they had become hostile, bitter enemies. But my dad said, "You go to Washington anyway! That son of a bitch told me that he would take care of you, and I want to see if he's good for his word."

I said, "I'm just supposed to walk in and announce that I am here and that he promised?"

"Absolutely! You walk right in there and say, 'We are holding you to your commitment.'" [laughter] So I did.

I won't repeat McCarran's language, but after he de-
nounced my father roundly he said, "I promised him, and
here you are, so I'll give you a job and help you get into law
school."

In the fall of 1941 I started law school. Although I would
have been satisfied to go to just about any school, I had been
accepted at George Washington, which was considered pretty
good in those days. Grades earned as an undergraduate
weren't as important for admission as they are today, and if
you had the money it was easier to get in. Of course, I had
some help from Senator McCarran, and influence was more
important then than it is now, as far as admission to a school
was concerned. It wouldn't have been unusual for Senator
McCarran to call up the dean of a law school and say, "I have
a fine young man from Nevada who is going to apply. See
what you can do." He held tremendous power.

McCarran had at least fifty Nevadans in Washington under
his patronage over the years that he was a senator . . .
maybe more. Many of them are still around, and we are all
close friends. We were known as the "McCarran Boys," and
I was called that when I ran for governor. McCarran was so
powerful: he was chairman of the senate judiciary committee
during his later years; he was second in seniority on the
appropriations committee; he was chairman of the District of
Columbia committee (they don't have that anymore), and that
made him mayor of D.C. So he had jobs all over the place
that he could put Nevada students in, and he did. I was a
Capitol Hill cop the first year I was under his patronage, and
my only instructions were to do nothing. [laughter] You just
sat there, and if something happened you called a certain
number. It was perfect for a student, because you worked at
night, had a nice desk and a lamp, and you could sit and
study for eight hours. It was terrific! A great many Nevadans,
including Harry Reid, did that.

Senator Patrick A. McCarran
*"I accepted what he offered me, and I had absolutely no hesitation
about repaying my debt."*

Lt. Grant Sawyer, 1945

"I was afraid I would lose my glasses and wouldn't be able to see, so I carried several extra sets . . . in my cartridge belt, my pockets and elsewhere."

I attended law school for one year before entering military service. Because my eyes were very bad and I couldn't pass the eye exams, I wasn't drafted, but I was so sensitive about not being in . . . . Everybody else was in, and I considered my failure degrading, so I kept applying to any branch — I didn't care which — and finally was accepted by the army. They may have been getting down to the dregs at that point, and were taking more people than they had previously. [laughter]

From Reno I went to Fort Douglas in Utah, where I was inducted and did my basic training. After basic I was held over in what they called "cadre," which was headquarters staff who gave inductees their basic training. Eventually I was transferred to Camp Robertson, Arkansas, where I was also cadre. By that time I was a corporal. While stationed at Camp Robertson I was sent to William and Mary College for advanced training in administrative matters, some of which I had already been handling, such as personnel. From there I went to Camp Fannin, Texas, in the same capacity, and began trying to get into officers candidate school (OCS). Initially I was unable to pass the eye exam, but I eventually memorized some charts, and, if I knew which chart they were using, I figured I could breeze through it, no problem. [laughter] Finally I got a chart that I knew, passed the physical at Camp Fannin and wound up in OCS at Camp Lee, Virginia. After about three months, I came out a second lieutenant. (Camp Lee was a quartermaster school, so I was no longer assigned to the infantry.)

Following OCS I went to the Philippines on a troop-replacement ship. There were a lot of old guys that I shipped over with who were physically deficient, like myself. (They were taking people by that time up into their early forties, I think. None of us, I would say, was the cream of the crop!) I was so blind that I was afraid I would get into some kind of situation and lose my glasses and wouldn't be able to see, and that could have been a total disaster. So I carried several extra sets of glasses on me . . . in my cartridge belt, my pockets and elsewhere. The army didn't care whether you were in the quartermaster corps or what you were, you went where the action was, and I was put in charge of an infantry squad. Most of the people in my group weren't prepared to go into battle at all, but, nevertheless, there we were in a Philippine battle zone. There were a lot of booby traps and that sort of thing, and there were caves with Japanese soldiers still in them. We also encountered sporadic gunfire in the suburbs of Manila, where we conducted sort of a cleaning-up operation. For about a week we bivouacked out next to a rice paddy with our guns and equipment, and right across the paddy were the Japanese. It was a great relief to me when I got lucky and got out of there.

One day, a truck loaded with people came out from Manila. They sat down and started to interview everyone there for the Philippine Civil Affairs Unit (PCAU), which was in the headquarters group in Manila. I was one of two picked to go to the unit, and I spent the rest of my time in the Philippines in Manila. The Japanese had occupied the Philippines for some time, and the PCAU was supposed to restore government and transfer its functions back to the Filipino people. We went out to the POW camps in and around Manila, and freed the prisoners. Then I was placed in charge of a district of Manila; I was sort of the mayor or the governor of that whole district, and I ran the schools and did all the things that you were supposed to do for the government. We had Filipino clerks and accountants working for us, and I got to know a lot of Filipinos who were in the government. (I saw some of them in later years, either when I went there or they came here.)

One of the funny things that happened to me in my district involved an inspection tour of a school. GIs were lined up through the school's courtyard, and down about a block and a half. I thought, "What the hell is going on here?" Well, I discovered that I was running a major house of prostitution, unbeknownst to me until I followed the line all the way up to where the action was! I was forced to shut it down . . . against my will. [laughter]

You put in so much time, and you would get to go to a rest camp. Shortly before the end of the war I was sent to one in Baguio, northern Luzon. Since I was the only quartermaster officer there, I was put in charge of the kitchen — I knew nothing whatsoever about the kitchen, but that's the way things were in those days, and I had a sergeant who knew all about it. When the war was declared over, hundreds of troops just left the camp. Most of them were gone for several days, a week or more, and then gradually, one-by-one, they wandered back and were accounted for. It was the strangest thing — people just left the camp and went into Manila and got drunk or something! But I couldn't leave because of my heavy responsibilities as the mess officer.

All told, I was in the Philippines for about a year. We had been scheduled to go to Japan for the expected invasion, but from Manila we were redirected to Korea, where I filled somewhat the same sort of role in Seoul as I had in Manila. The Japanese had occupied Korea for forty years, and they owned and controlled everything, so when the war ended and they left, the Koreans were totally unprepared for independence. Our unit moved in and set up a transition kind of government, with our barracks in back of the city hall. It was summer when we arrived, and the army had not taken into consideration the seasonal change that would occur in the climate. Winters in Korea are very severe with a lot of snow, extremely cold, but the only uniforms we had were summer khakis, short-sleeved Filipino dress; and when winter came we had to wear two or three layers of khaki pants or whatever we could find, because we never were issued winter uniforms! Nor were we given any language lessons.

A military government is supposed to speak the language of the country that it is helping through transition, but the army had not taught us Korean — I couldn't speak any at all, and the officer who was with me couldn't either. Nonetheless, we were placed in charge of selling some Japanese-owned assets to Korean civilians. The only way we could communicate with Koreans was through interpreters (we had three or four), but we bumbled along and interviewed the Korean civilians that would come in to buy this house or that plot of land, or whatever asset was on the block. It finally dawned on me that there was something going on that I didn't understand. We operated out of a museum (which is still there), and these people would come in, sit down for an interview, and the interpreter would talk to them for maybe ten minutes. When they were through, I would say to the interpreter, "What did he say?" And he would tell me that he had said, "Good morning." It finally dawned on my partner and me that each deal had been discussed and made, and the asset sold, before we ever learned what was going on. It was a done thing by the time they turned to us, and the friends of the interpreters got very good deals. That was just an example of what can happen in a turbulent wartime situation.

I was in Korea for a year, but don't have much sense of accomplishment about being there. We were frustrated at our inability to do the job that we were supposed to do — the army didn't provide competent help in that transition period, but we did the best we could.

We were discharged from service in those days based on points — they would calculate how many you had, and when you reached a certain number you were eligible for discharge. I had to wait about a year after the war was over to be discharged, and, although there was never any doubt in my mind that I would return to law school when I got out of the service, there were times when I thought I would never get out! [laughter] Still, even though it was a much longer period than I would have liked, I consider the four years that I spent in the service the most valuable four years of my life. There were so many things you had to learn in order to survive in the service — you had to learn to share; to test yourself physically, maybe more than mentally; to relate to people that were the kind of people that you had never met or been around before, both racial and otherwise. You had to learn how to survive; you had to develop a kind of philosophy that enabled you, no matter how bad things got, to cope. No matter how frightened you were, you had to learn that things were probably going to get better, and you couldn't control any of those things anyway — somebody else controlled them. I've always believed since then that compulsory military service is a good idea. That learning experience gives people a chance to grow up, and it exposes them to different cultures that they otherwise might never encounter. It also tests people individually. Somebody would say, "Today we go on a fifteen-mile hike and you're carrying a pack of forty pounds." There was no way! Then, much to your amazement, you did; it just about killed you, but you did it.

Being in the service also taught me how to handle people. When I first went in, I was extremely reluctant to take orders from sergeants who I thought probably couldn't even read or write: get up at five o'clock in the morning, and do this or do that, and I'm thinking, "Who is this son of a bitch to tell *me* what to do?" I never had been particularly able to handle authority anyway, but I had to learn that those virtual illiterates had a place, too. I learned that they can be very good at what they do, maybe a lot better than I could, even though I considered myself somewhat superior in terms of background and education. Those people all had a place, and it was a very important place that I didn't really understand before. Of course, I was about twenty when I went in, and I had a lot to learn. But you learn fast there if you are going to survive. I came out of the service a totally different person. I was much more mature, a great deal more understanding of the other person's point of view, and I count that as a great positive experience in my life. Of course, I wasn't killed, I wasn't injured, and any deprivations that I suffered were in my best interests.

Notwithstanding the many people who complain about their war experiences, how terrible they were — and, I am sure they were for many people — I think the generation that came out of World War II was probably one of the most productive generations that this country has ever seen. We felt we had lost time, so we had to hurry, we had to accomplish things reasonably fast after we got out.

I was discharged in California and came to Nevada to stay at my father's home. My old fraternity at the University of Nevada was having a party, and my college roommate, Carlisle Pribbernow — who also had just been discharged from the service — contacted me and arranged a blind date for me with his cousin, Bette. The party was quite a strain, because it was a drunken ATO costume party, and Bette had a bad cold and could barely talk. (My daughter informs me that that kind of party is still held at the University of Nevada.) Bette got into this with me and all my old friends, and she felt quite neglected . . . plus,

I could never remember her name, and I had to keep asking her. She recounts that story frequently. I thought our date was fine, but she didn't think so. [laughter]

Before I went back to law school we had more dates, virtually every night, and when I went back to school I wrote to Bette and asked her to marry me. Her parents had only met me a couple of times, and they were somewhat shocked at the rapidity of the whole thing. When they got to Washington for the wedding, it was sort of a confused situation. I had called around looking for a Baptist minister (Bette was also a Baptist), but the ministers were all out of town on summer vacation. I finally found one guy who said that he would come back to town to marry us, and he gave me the address of his church.

When Bette and her parents arrived, we got into the taxi to go to the church, and I gave the driver the address, and he said to us, "Are you sure this is where you want to go?"

We said, "Well, this is the address. We are going to get married." I didn't really know the minister; I had just talked to him on the phone. Bette's parents got a little bit worried as we proceeded toward the wedding. [laughter] We were right in the heart of the blackest section of Washington, D.C.

We were married August 1, 1946, and Bette immediately looked for a job and got one with a cancer clinic. Then she went to work at the Academy of Sciences in a very good job which she kept until we left Washington. Bette was making more money than I was. I was only making ninety dollars a month with Senator McCarran, but I had the GI Bill.

It had been a mixed-up four years since I completed my first year at George Washington. After the war I transferred to Georgetown, which was a better law school, but I got caught right in the middle of a chaotic situation. For example, I took Real Property II before Real Property I, which was insane, but that's the way the courses fell. My classes were at night and sometimes on mornings, and there was nothing about it that was orderly; and I'd missed four years and the world was passing me by, and my desire was just to get this over and get out. Although my grades were pretty good — much better than they had been in college — I certainly didn't come out of law school a great lawyer, I'll tell you that! I graduated in 1948 after a year and a half (it should have taken two), and then I took the District of Columbia bar exam.

During my stint in law school after the war, I worked once again as a support person in Senator McCarran's office. Eva Adams was the ruler of the office in those days, and I would do whatever she told me to do, but mostly I worked with veterans: helping people who were being held without cause to get released from the army, and trying to take care of bereaved mothers and wives and those who wanted their spouses or sons back from the service . . . assisting veterans with pension problems. I would deal with the bureaus that handled those things, usually in Senator McCarran's name.

Eva Adams was an extremely gracious, wonderfully bright person who obviously was in charge of McCarran's office, and during those years she was a power in the Senate in her own right: the organization representing senate secretaries and administrative assistants was very strong, and she was president of that group during one of the years that I was there. Eva was the most efficient, most sophisticated woman that I had ever run into, and we were all in awe of her. She was the hostess; she was the chairman; she was the person in charge of all things — everything cleared through Eva, and your assignments were from Eva. Most of us did not even see the senator very often because Eva guarded him and pro-tected him zealously, and I'm sure that was his desire. A couple of people other than Eva were also reasonably close to McCarran, but primarily in a professional way. Cal Cory (later an attorney in Las Vegas), was one of McCarran's chief legislative assistants, and he was involved in all the senator's campaigns. Jay Sourwine, a real intellectual, was McCarran's chief executive assistant on the senate judiciary committee.

The senator was an able man. One time when I was assigned to attend to him on the Senate floor there was a debate on a policy matter, and he was bucking the administration, which he sometimes did. I am not sure what the issue was, but Florida Senator Claude Pepper was supposed to have been with him, and the two of them were to lead the fight on the Senate floor. Pepper ducked out, though, and left McCarran all by himself. The debate started at three o'clock in the afternoon, with McCarran the only person leading the fight on his side, and he was then getting fairly well along in age. At four o'clock the next morning the opposition finally gave up. They never got to the question. He was so clever, so smart, that just on parliamentary maneuvers he held the debate up until they all finally got tired and gave up and went home. That proved to me that here was a man who was so able intellectually, who would question him?

Senator McCarran treated us all with respect, and he certainly was nice to me, although I'm sure that from his perspective I was just another one of those kids that were out there working in the office doing something . . . maybe he wasn't even sure what! We all looked upon him as the Holy Ghost: we thought anything he did was just terrific, and none of us McCarran Boys really questioned his policies, not even in private. We were in a sort of orbit where the senator was the center of everything . . . we totally lost perspective. I later found the same thing to be true among my own people when I was governor: they didn't question me; they were just proud to be part of my team.

In the Senate McCarran wasn't so beloved, but he was
highly respected because he was bright, persuasive, eloquent,
dogged and vindictive. (If you didn't go along with the
senator, at some point you were going to pay.) He was
tremendously powerful in his own right, and he had formed
a coalition with southern senators who had been there all
their lives. Other senators understood what he could do from
his positions in the judiciary and appropriations committees,
in particular, and knew that they just couldn't afford to be his
enemies. If you had the power to trade favors with other
senators, then you were in a position of great influence, and
Senator McCarran certainly did!

We were all pretty young then, and I was proud to be
called a McCarran Boy, and I still am; I don't have any
reservations about that at all. But after you leave that atmosphere (Washington, D.C., and McCarran's office) and get out
on your own, you begin to develop and mature, and you may
discover that you have philosophical differences. That's what
happened to me and a lot of other people. As I began to
understand the senator's politics and his personal proclivities,
I came to the realization that he held many of the same deep
social and racial biases that my father and so many others
held at that time. Some of the legislation that he passed was
later thought to be discriminatory, particularly his immigration
legislation, and he was very protectionist — although he was
not a McCarthyite, communists became almost an obsession
with him. I eventually concluded that he was a person who
did not hold the same kind of democratic feeling about all
human beings that I thought I did.

There were a great many
young men from Nevada whom the senator helped: Alan
Bible was one; Virgil Wedge in Reno; Clark Guild and Dyer

Jensen, both attorneys in Reno; Ralph Denton in Las Vegas, and his brother, Lew; Bill Morris, another attorney in Las Vegas. There were so many of them . . . . There are probably thirty or forty men still alive who went through "the McCarran School." But some of the McCarran Boys did not later come through for the senator in turn, and frankly I always thought that they were sort of traitors: after all, he took care of us! Whatever personal feelings we might have had, we owed him. I had accepted what he offered me, and I had absolutely no hesitation about repaying my debt, and that was my feeling until the day he died. In later years we may have had our philosophical and political differences, but that doesn't have anything to do with the fact that he was my mentor, and I will never be apologetic for any association with him. In his way McCarran was a great man, one of the most outstanding public figures ever to come out of the state of Nevada.

3

---

law or politics ?

After completing law school I wanted to return to Nevada, but I really didn't know anybody in the state except a few people from the university, and my father and some of his colleagues, and constituents whom I had met while working in Senator McCarran's office. Nobody was particularly interested in me; they had never heard of me, by-and-large. However, I did have the advantage of being a Patrick McCarran protégé.

As a McCarran Boy, once you returned to Nevada there was sort of an understanding (primarily with Eva) that you would be for the senator and work to perpetuate him in office. That was just understood. I won't say that this was carefully calculated, but they wanted to have strong McCarran people in every community, and upon returning to Nevada the McCarran Boys were to locate in areas where the senator and his people needed help politically. It was suggested that I go to Ely. With no other particular destination in mind, Bette and I started out from Las Vegas in our old Chevy to tour the state. We would make the circuit, and I would stop in every town, starting with Ely, and talk to attorneys.

While in Ely I talked to Dutch Horton, who was practicing law there. He had been one of my predecessors in McCarran's office, a McCarran Boy who had been in Washington about the same time that Alan Bible was. Dutch had returned to Ely, and he was considered part of the McCarran machine there all his natural life — although he never ran for public office, he served on a lot of state committees and various appointive things. He had a very successful law practice, and he never needed to be a district attorney or anything else. Dutch was, I would say, the most prominent citizen in Ely for a good many years. (Dutch Horton later became a real ally of mine, and we worked together on a lot of political things. I usually appointed him parliamentarian when I was heading a convention. He had an understanding of how these things were to be handled — with a quick gavel. We called it "Horton's Rules of Order." [laughter])

It so happened that my wife and I had gotten to Ely the day of a big storm, and that night a great slide came down. The main street was a sea of mud the next morning, and the whole thing was so depressing that we thought we'd move on. From Ely we went to Elko, where there were twelve attorneys. They were all very nice; I didn't know a soul there, but it seemed like a nice town. From there we went across to Battle Mountain, Winnemucca, Lovelock, stopping in each town, and then on to Reno. There, we decided that Elko was where we were going to go, so we packed up the old Chevy and went back to Elko, and that was it!

Elko was a community of six thousand people with about nine thousand in the whole county. It was a ranching community, and most of the people — even the ones who lived in town — were from second, third, or fourth generation Elko County families . . . old families that in an odd way were quite sophisticated. Most of them had money, and many had traveled throughout the world, as well as in the United States. Naturally, because it had a small, close-knit population, Elko was a difficult community to break into. A newcomer might have a bit of a problem gaining acceptance, but my relationship with Pat McCarran made it easier for us, because Mrs. McCarran's sister lived in Elko and her daughter had been in school with me at the University of Nevada. They were prominent citizens, and they sort of took us in and eased the way for us into social life. We've seen other people who had to live there fifteen years before they were even invited to a bridge party. [laughter]

Those Nevadans whose law schooling had been interrupted by service in World War II were exempt from taking the state bar exam, and I was the twelfth and last attorney to be admitted under that rule. (Although I had already passed the Washington, D.C., bar exam, there was no reciprocity with Nevada, so that didn't count.) To set up a practice in Elko, I borrowed two thousand dollars from my dad. There was an old gal whose deceased husband had practiced law in Elko County for years, and she still had his library; I bought that from her for a pittance, and I rented an office in the First National Bank. We also rented a little apartment, but in 1949, when our daughter Gail was born, we had to move out, so I went to Chris Sheerin — the editor of the *Elko Daily Free Press*, a Republican newspaper — and he, without a note or anything, loaned me enough money to buy a little house. Chris later became a close friend of mine.

I didn't have very many clients in the beginning, but Grant is a big name in the Mormon church, and there are a lot of Mormon people in Elko, so I was the beneficiary of that —

even though there were a couple of LDS attorneys in Elko, many people thought that I was LDS, and they came to me as a brother Mormon. That didn't last too long, because they gradually became aware that I *wasn't*. [laughter] Then I just got people off the street and whoever. We survived. As a matter of fact, I think we paid my dad his two thousand dollars back during the first year.

In my law practice I would take all types of cases, and shortly after I started that got me into an extremely uncomfortable situation. Alex Puccinelli, the very popular district attorney, was a good-looking, bright and articulate fellow who had been mentioned for major public office a number of times. He sent a case to me, which I took, and I signed all the pleadings. Much to my astonishment, when I got into court there was Mr. Puccinelli on the other side representing the other party! I was young and didn't understand what was happening, so I told the judge, Taylor Wines, what had occurred. Nothing had been signed by Mr. Puccinelli (it was all signed by me), and he denied that he had ever been involved with my client and the case; but the client had gone to him and considered him the attorney. The issue of conflict of interest created a terrible flap which ended in the disbarment of Mr. Puccinelli, whom I liked, and I was sorry about the whole mess. I was new in town, it was an extremely embarrassing and uncomfortable situation, and I felt sort of guilty creating that much trouble for a man who was held in such high regard. (Oddly enough, when Mr. Puccinelli died his widow came to me to handle his estate, which I did.)

Snowy Monroe, the editor of the weekly *Elko Independent*, was a Democrat who was active locally in party politics, and I got to know him shortly after I moved to Elko. There was a little age difference

— he was maybe ten years older — but we became good friends, and Snowy was a great supporter of mine all the way through my political career. He was, if anything, a little embarrassing occasionally when he would overdo his praise of me, but he was always in my corner, and in Elko that was very significant because most of the money and the power were Republican — it always took a valiant effort to get Democrats elected to office. Snowy ultimately ran for state senator and represented Elko County until the reapportionment of 1964.

In a little town like Elko, where you all have to live together, you don't let politics interfere with friendships — personal relationships and reputations mean more than party labels, and you don't go to the mat just because you are a Democrat or a Republican. The principal Republican in Elko was Newt Crumley, who later was in the state senate, and he was a very classy guy. In fact some of my best friends there were Republicans . . . and they are friends to this day, as far as I'm concerned. We sort of understood one another's positions and let it go at that: I would vote all the Democratic names, I was Democratic chairman of the county and went through all the steps, but that didn't make any difference in my friendships. As a matter of fact, they were all avid supporters of mine when I ran for DA, even though most of them were Republicans.

When I ran for DA in 1950 against Leo Puccinelli, Alex Puccinelli's cousin, I had no idea that I could get elected; I just ran. I hadn't been in Elko long enough to be very well known, and my father thought that I was running too early . . . that I should wait and go through the steps. But my newness may have worked to my advantage. The Puccinelli family went back three generations in the county, and in that time they had, of course, made a few enemies and become the objects of some jealousy and resentment. I was new and fresh, and the voters were looking for somebody new, and I campaigned very hard and covered the whole county and did all the things you were supposed to do. That's about the only way to account for my victory. It was almost embarrassing the way it turned out: I was elected by a margin of more than four to one.

When I became district attorney the DA's office was a one-man operation, with a secretary. My office was in the county courthouse along with the judge, the library, the county clerk, and the other elected officials. Later I requested a deputy, and the county commissioners denied it; but by studying the law I came to the conclusion that even though they would not consent, I had the power to hire a deputy myself. Of course, they had the power to decide whether or not he would be paid! [laughter] So a after a while I did take on a deputy, Ralph Denton, who is now practicing in Las Vegas. Ralph had graduated from law school about 1950, and he came to Elko and signed on as my unpaid deputy. He did it for the love of the job, no doubt. [laughter] Actually, I paid him out of my own salary just to establish the precedent. I was making about nine thousand dollars a year, and I paid Ralph out of what I was making, so that's how the deputy DA position became established in Elko County. About a year passed before the county commissioners finally broke loose and paid him a little stipend of some kind.

I had met Ralph through his brother, Lew Denton, who was my roommate when I was in law school in Washington. Ralph is about eight years younger than Lew. (They're from Caliente, and I knew their parents. Their father was the under sheriff of Lincoln County, and their mother was a school-teacher and was very bright.) Lew and I roomed together during my first year of law school; then we all went into the service and came back. After the war, while I was working in McCarran's office, Ralph was in Washington in the army. I no longer was rooming with his brother, but we all wound up in a sort of rooming house together with some other Nevadans and close friends.

Ralph was a very gregarious, outgoing guy. He was perfectly charming, and we got to be good friends. Bette and I kept trying to fix him up with various girls, but it was after we left Washington that he married Sara, who was a very high class Washington administrative-secretary type. When they moved to Elko we became quite close because we shared the DA's office. (Their first child was born in Elko and became good friends with Gail.) Then Ralph decided to go into private practice, and he went into an office with Jack Robbins, the senator from Elko at that time. He practiced with him for two or three years, then went on to Las Vegas.

While I was district attorney I was allowed to keep my private practice, so I was handling cases both as DA and as a private lawyer. (The salary just wasn't sufficient to live on, so they permitted DAs in those days to have a private practice to supplement their income. As long as there wasn't a conflict of interest, it was OK.) I would go in as "Mr. Sawyer" one day, and be prosecuting for the people the next. [laughter] That's still the way it is in some counties in Nevada. I much preferred my private defense work to prosecution, because my natural inclinations were always for the underdog and I had had some defense practice before becoming district attorney. But the thrill of the combat, whether you are defense or prosecution, is always exciting. The contest of wits is invigorating for anybody, and I enjoyed it very much.

The duties and responsibilities of the Elko DA's office were much the same as any other district attorney's office: prosecute criminal cases, civil cases . . . defend the city and the county. Initially I had to do it all myself, and there was a lot of work, particularly if I got into a major murder trial or something like that. (I had several of those.) Consequently I didn't have much time for civil practice, but it was a very useful experience. It's good for any young lawyer fresh out of school to join a public defender's office or a district attorney's office.

I loved trial work, particularly arguing a case before a jury, and I did an awful lot of that during the eight years that I was district attorney. It was sort of like law school: the things that I was interested in, I did pretty well at. Other things, bankruptcies and that kind of thing, I was not at all interested in . . . and still am not. [laughter] All the time spent in court gave me experience that was extremely helpful to me as a litigator later on. You're thrown into the breach before you really know what it's all about, but there's no one but you to do it, so you can't hide behind anybody. In criminal practice, particularly, you take it as it comes; win or lose, it's your responsibility. It's marvelous training if you can stand it — you are humiliated by the terrible mistakes you make, and you're the subject of criticism because you don't know what you're doing. Learning how to handle yourself in court is a very tough thing for a young lawyer to do! You have a judge, who is a superior personage, looking down at you, and you're contesting with experienced lawyers on the other side who know what they are doing. If you can get through that, then you are ready to cope with almost anything in the practice of law. After ten years of practicing in Elko, I felt I could get along in almost any court. I had lost that terrible fear of embarrassment.

My relationship with the law enforcement people in Elko County was good. The sheriff was a friend of mine, we worked together well, and neither of us was trying to outdo the other in coverage or publicity. [laughter] Whether to prosecute or not was always pretty much a matter of my own judgment, and I was never challenged on that. If the sheriff brought to me someone who had committed a crime, I had the latitude to sit down and work things out if I felt it was something frivolous.

Plea bargaining was handled much more informally in those days than now — I would work with the defendant, and often the case never went to court. I felt that in many cases you could do more good by handling certain matters some way other than through incarceration. Prison is a debilitating experience — there is virtually nothing positive about it — and I was in the fortunate position of being able to influence the decision about who went and who didn't. Somebody once brought to me a local boy who had been exposing himself around the community. Since I had the latitude of sitting down and talking to him, we put together a program where he would go to Salt Lake City and have a psychiatric evaluation. I wanted him to work out his problems, if possible, without my having to file a charge (which I didn't) and he's now one of the leading citizens of Elko County. It was a matter of judgment. Now district attorneys are much more under the gun. They feel they have to prosecute — it's kind of a macho thing. You see this particularly in some of the city court proceedings and many district court proceedings in Nevada. It's my view that many of the these cases should never have been brought to court; it's a waste of taxpayers' money because it doesn't help either the general public or the defendant, who may have just made a mistake.

People weren't as judgmental in those days as they are now, particularly if you were dealing with one of your own. People were much more forgiving. The first experience that I had in prosecuting a murder case was a lady who had killed her husband. It was open and shut, first degree murder, no

question about it. But everybody in the community hated that
man so badly that it only took the jury about thirty seconds
to acquit the defendant, and it was a first-class murder case!
They were ready to give the lady a medal. She was a heroine.
[laughter] Although you have a solid case, it doesn't necessarily mean that the case should be tried. There's not much
sense in trying a case that you can't win. I never was in favor
of capital punishment, and I don't know that a good district
attorney should have that feeling; nevertheless, I prosecuted
three or four people who did get the death sentence,
although I didn't ask for it. In fact, in one case I asked them
not to return the death sentence, but they did anyway.

There were three basic legal or law enforcement issues in
the Elko County public's mind at that time: juvenile delinquency was a problem in city schools; locally, Indian rights
was an issue; and communism was thought to be a threat.
However, there isn't a lot a district attorney is going to be
able to do about communism — anti-communism was merely
part of the political rhetoric of the day, and I presumed that
most people who were running for office had to be against
communism. [laughter] On the juvenile delinquency issue,
there was some in Elko, but I don't suppose any more than
in most communities. Indians were another matter, because
in Elko County there is quite a large Indian reservation at
Owyhee, on the Idaho-Nevada border.

The way Indians were treated in Elko and generally
throughout the country was disgraceful, in my opinion, and
I thought that not only had we in many cases illegally stolen
their lands and their properties, but we had made them wards
of the government through a very inept agency — the Bureau
of Indian Affairs. We dole out just enough money to them in
Nevada so that they don't have to work; and in Elko they had
a terrible alcohol problem because most of them *didn't* work.
The wives worked as housemaids around town, but the males

Young District Attorney Grant Sawyer *(left)* in an Elko Little Theater production.

Gail Sawyer, 1954
" . . . the one constant joy of our lives since her birth."

didn't work, and we gave them enough money to stay drunk, and that was about the end of it — we took no further responsibility. I felt very seriously about that issue and have never changed my view on that. As a nation, I think we bungled the whole Indian problem about as badly as we could have.

One Elko community project in which I was involved was the Silver Stage Players, a little theater group. I had been very active in little theater work in college and even in the army — in fact, we formed a little theater in Little Rock, Arkansas, when I was in the army. We did a show called *Texas Yank*, which we wrote, produced, and acted in, and we traveled in some of the southern states for one of the bond drives during the war. (We raised a lot of money.) That had been sort of my thing, so when we moved to Elko I got together with a group of other people in town and we formed a little theater and produced a number of plays. (That little theater is still going.) I played Mr. Massoula in *Father of the Bride*, and in 1954 I helped direct the play, *Laura*, which was a lot of fun. Anything you enjoy, like I did acting, is a break from the routine of whatever you're doing, and I was in all the plays in those years that I was there. I love acting, but I never had any time for it after Elko.

We lived in Elko when we were young, and we were among a group of people our own age. We were there for ten years, and our daughter Gail was born there and went to school there. That's the only place we've been long enough to establish close relationships. Elko was a wonderful community, and many of the closest friends we have in the world still live there.

My interests were sort
of balanced between the law and politics — I enjoyed the
more dramatic aspects of practicing law, and the theatricality
of politics attracted me too. The 1952 Nevada state Democratic convention was held in Wells, and I was the representative from Elko. Although I had been in the state for only
about four years and was not a big wheel in the party — not
even an insider in Democratic politics statewide — I was
elected chairman of the convention: I was a McCarran Boy!
[laughter] That convention was predominantly right-to-work
in sentiment, and as chairman I presided over it and
supported the right-to-work side. Jim "Sailor" Ryan, the labor
leader from Las Vegas, led the opposition. Ryan was abrasive,
clever, and smart. On several occasions he challenged my
rulings, and we had to put them to a vote, but I tried to keep
things moving while acting in an impartial manner. When
chairing conventions, whether or not I agreed with the
proponents of certain positions, I treated them fairly. We
always figured we had the votes anyway.

Senator George Smathers of Florida was the featured
speaker at the 1952 convention. He had probably been
invited by McCarran, who controlled the state Democratic
machine. (In fact McCarran and some of his cronies in Reno
were virtually non-partisan — to a certain extent they
controlled the thinking of *both* parties.) The conservative
McCarran Democrats were obsessed with ferreting out
Americans who were "soft on communism," and asking
Smathers to speak was a natural expression of that.[1] While
under McCarran's tutelage in Washington I had uncritically
accepted such positions at face value, but by the time of this
convention I was developing a real antipathy to the witch
hunt; and, repelled by it, I eventually became convinced that
it was the worst sort of purely political charlatanism . . .

similar to the American flag gambit employed by George Bush when he ran for president in 1988: phony, and with no redeeming merit. The whole McCarthy thing was reprehensible;[2] unfortunately, McCarran, in effect, was part of it, as was Richard Nixon.

In September of 1954 Senator McCarran died of a heart attack in Hawthorne. It took me completely by surprise. Over Democratic objections that McCarran's empty seat should be put on the November ballot, Ernest Brown was appointed by Governor Russell to serve out the remaining two years of Senator McCarran's term. Finally, however, the Nevada supreme court had to say yes, the seat should be on the ballot, and the Democrats can contest it.[3] Immediately the scramble started over who we would nominate to succeed McCarran in the Senate.

I had been elected chairman of the Elko County Democratic Central Committee to succeed Jack Robbins, who had died the month before, and then I was elected to the state central committee and I was serving on it at the time of McCarran's death. (Robbins had been *the* Democrat in Elko County, a McCarran man, highly regarded and respected not only in Elko, but also in the state senate, which he had dominated regardless of which party was in control. Jack Robbins had been the senior state senator for many, many years.) As a member of the central committee I was involved in several meetings, one in particular in Carson City, in which we discussed who the party should put forward for the U.S. Senate seat. Alan Bible, the former state attorney general, was the natural choice to succeed Senator McCarran, and he did eventually become the Democratic nominee . . . and a senator.[4] A number of other people would have loved to have had the nomination, of course, but Bible was the predominant figure in those discussions.

In 1956 I was a delegate to the Democratic National
Convention, and I served on the resolutions committee.
Senator Bible flew to Chicago from Nevada where he was
campaigning, and he and I drafted a strong plank to protect
western mining. (Alan knew a lot more about mining than I
did, so his input was much more important than mine.)
Mining was really suffering from Republican policy in those
years. Once the Korean War had ended, Eisenhower with-
drew supports for stockpiling strategic metals and minerals, of
which Nevada has a great many, and in our draft we empha-
sized the need for such supports. It was up to me to lobby
the resolution through the committee, but the other delegates
didn't give a damn about mining, by and large, so it took a
little politicking to get what we wanted; but after forming a
coalition of delegates from the western states, I got support
from others in the committee, and we handled the whole
thing so successfully that I don't believe there was even a
minority report on that particular plank. For many years I
remained on the resolutions and platform committee, which
I felt was the most important national committee. In those
days each state was entitled to one person on each committee: one for the resolutions and platform; one for bylaws; one
for each other committee. Now it's a one-man, one-vote thing,
where Nevada may have one person on a committee and
California may have twenty. Consequently, Nevada has lost its
influence in the national party.

At their 1958 state convention Nevada's Democrats voted
to abolish the unit rule, which some counties had adopted for
their delegations. It was a rule which specified that an entire
delegation's votes were determined by a majority of the
delegation on any motion, resolution, or election of candidates. Of course, when all of the votes of a large delegation
could be controlled by just 51 percent of its members, the will
of the convention was thrown out of balance . . . it was not

accurately reflected in the final vote tally. The unit rule gave inordinate, and undemocratic, power to the largest counties.

Aligned with the small and northern counties on the question, I was right in the middle of it — in fact, I was the chairman of the convention. A very bitter fight developed, revolving around Clark County, which looked at the proposal as a move to break its power. In this potentially uneven struggle we employed what was later referred to as the "Sawyer Rules of Procedure": when we took the vote on whether or not to abolish the rule, the question was, "Will those counties that have the unit rule be able to use it in the vote that challenges its legitimacy?" [laughter] Clark County had come to the convention with a divided delegation, so that led to some very interesting parliamentary maneuvering. (Dutch Horton was my parliamentarian, and he called all the right shots!)

B_y 1956 I thought I could do both law and politics — if politics came along, I certainly wasn't averse to that, and I had the feeling that I could do both. At the time there was considerable turbulence on campus at the University of Nevada. The university's president, Minard Stout, was attempting to stifle freedom of speech and freedom of movement among his faculty — he had fired a professor who had taken an opposing position and gone to the legislature to express it.[5] I felt that Stout was being protected in his totalitarian stance by the board of regents, and that to correct the situation there needed to be some changes in the membership of the board. A number of my friends and acquaintances who were involved in the dispute convinced me that there probably was no one else to mount an effective challenge, so I decided to try for a seat on the university's board of regents in 1956 in the belief that if you are going to beef and complain about a situation, you should do something about it as well!

Election to the regents was by a statewide vote in those days — each candidate had to run throughout the state — and one of the candidates I ran against was Archie Grant, who was from Clark County. The vote was close enough so that it was two or three days before they decided who had won, and the ultimate outcome was that Archie Grant and Fred Anderson were elected. There had been some confusion surrounding the names Archie Grant and Grant Sawyer, and Archie always contended in a friendly way that the reason that I even ran as well as I did was because people thought they were voting for him. I turned that around, of course, and said the reason he won a seat was because people thought they were voting for me! [laughter] The board was soon expanded to nine members, and Governor Russell appointed me to a place on it. I remained on the board long enough to see Minard Stout fired in 1957, and then I resigned. I had decided to run for higher office.

4

running against the
establishment: 1958

There was a lot of speculation in 1958 about whether I would make a try for state office . . . and if so, which one? Governor Charles Russell, it was conceded, would run for a third term, but what Democrat would oppose him? Would it be me? There was talk about me not only for governor, but for attorney general, and for other offices like the United States Senate or House of Representatives. It covered the field.

E. L. Cord[1] and his associates were sort of successors to the McCarran machine. By 1958 they were pretty well running things in our party, and in some respects in the Republican party as well . . . shades of many years ago when George Wingfield was running everything in both parties! Fred Anderson,[2] some University of Nevada professors, and I were members of a dissatisfied rump group (for lack of a better term) of Nevada Democrats — the anti-Cords — who were opposed to one man and his cronies having such control over the state. When we got together to talk things over, my thinking went the same as it had when I had run for regent: we had no right to complain about a situation if we weren't willing to try to do something about it. So we decided that rather than simply commiserate with one another, we would put forward candidates for some of the offices that would be contested in the fall elections. Fred Anderson, it was decided, would try for the United States Senate nomination, and many people around the state also seemed to want me to run for something. My father thought I should run for attorney general, but our group wasn't much interested in that office. I didn't make up my mind until driving from Reno to Carson City to file for office: I filed for governor.

W̱e in the anti-Cord group thought of ourselves as progressives. Certainly we were not representative of the old guard — ours was a more liberal social agenda than either Democratic or Republican politics had advocated in this state up to that time. In our group were a number of professors and other people like Hazel Erskine[3] who were socially progressive and willing to stand up and say so, which took some courage in those days. The basis of our movement was really that we wanted change, and Cord's people didn't. They were almost bipartisan, in that to them politics was more a question of control than it was partisanship. They were powerful and influential people who found a common interest in running things in the state, from the legislature right on up through the governor and the congressional delegation.

Although I was a McCarran Boy, I wasn't uncomfortable about being the foe of a political machine that Pat McCarran had been partially responsible for establishing. Senator McCarran was dead by that time. Whether I would have felt so free had he still been alive, I don't know. [laughter] But Senator McCarran was no longer an issue, and I had never been close to Norman Biltz or E. L. Cord and the other people who were running this bipartisan control scheme . . . I didn't feel that my loyalty to McCarran necessarily had to transfer to his supporters. So we took on the machine.

In our number we included Tom Cooke (a Reno attorney and a dear friend of mine) and Bruce Barnum, who was from a small county and accepted the responsibility of organizing the little counties. Ralph Denton and Dick Ham were our primary people in the south, and then there was Graham Hollister, who was sort of a rancher-farmer dilettante who lived in Genoa. He was from a very wealthy California family that owned vast amounts of land — Hollister, California, was named after them. Graham was extremely liberal. He and Hazel and some of the professors were always out of step with Nevada on social issues, and I guess that's the reason they were attracted to my candidacy: they saw me as an opportunity for change. Graham didn't worry too much about either money or time, and he really just committed himself to our effort, even driving me all over the state on several occasions, campaigning. (I didn't have a car I could use for this, but he contributed his.) He was an interesting man, filled with enthusiasm, and he was devoted to me and vice versa.

Among the people in my campaign there was a common denominator: none were experienced political operatives. This was a whole new group who suddenly came into politics through me. They had not been heard of much in established political circles, and they were not the usual types that you would go to and say, "Look, I want to mount a campaign for office. Will you help me run it?" Ralph Denton was politically knowledgeable, but he wasn't an operative in the sense that he could pick people in Clark County to run a campaign. Dick Ham was new to the process, and I doubt he had ever been involved in a campaign before; and none of these people were paid — practically everybody volunteered, which today would be impossible. We were really a group of amateurs trying to put together an organization from scratch.

Even before I filed there were indications of support for us in most of the northern counties, and although I didn't know who would be filing against me, I began envisioning this as maybe a north-south contest, which indeed it did become. To win I figured I needed about 20 percent of Clark County, assuming that I would get the largest percentage of the northern votes, and that was the analysis of others who were involved in planning our strategy early on. Unfortunately, I didn't know many people in Las Vegas except some Democrats who were usually my adversaries at any Democratic convention. [laughter] And "Sailor" Jim Ryan and the labor group didn't have much regard for me at all. So as soon as the north began to shape up, I felt I had to find some way to cut into the Clark County vote.

Ralph Denton was willing to stick his neck out and try to organize our campaign in the south. Ralph and I had both been quite active in the party, and were always in the same conspiracies when it came to Democratic conventions. He was liberal and he was gutsy, and we were pretty much soul mates on political issues, but though he helped me a lot during that and later campaigns, he wasn't a Sawyer man — he's his own man. We remain extremely close, and as a matter of fact Ralph's daughter gave the name Grant to the son born to her in 1991. That pleased me very much. I have considered Ralph probably my closest friend all these years. (Richard Ham, who had a grocery store in Boulder City, was also involved in our campaign in the south. Richard was not

Grant Sawyer during the 1958 campaign
*"I had a crew cut. That projected an image of a young
man on the move, vigorous . . . . "*

a political heavyweight, but he was a bright, appealing guy, and in those days was considered extremely liberal.)

From the moment I filed on July 10, I came out swinging. My principal rival in the primary, Attorney General Harvey Dickerson, was a Cord ally, so I began attacking E. L. Cord and his machine, suggesting that they spoke only for a small group of wealthy, influential, bipartisan people who wanted the state to themselves. We adopted the corny slogan, "Nevada's not for sale," and poor Mr. Cord, who wasn't a candidate, suddenly was the issue of the campaign. I didn't even know the man, but I was using him as the symbol of my opposition to the group that had controlled the state for a great many years, and whether Dickerson was close to Cord or not, there was no question that he was the candidate of that group.

My platform in the primary was pro-labor, cheap water and power sources for industrial development, no new taxes, gaming control, and "Nevada's not for sale." One of my chief concerns was that gaming control was weak — that too many people were being granted licenses who shouldn't be, and that there was extensive organized crime control of the industry, particularly in Las Vegas. My position was that Nevada should be keeping the mob out from the beginning, rather than attempting to get them out after they had been licensed. I later learned that some of what I believed was based on rumor rather than fact, but I thought it was time to clamp down and take a tough position on gaming. We had to project an image to the rest of the country that Nevada was not rolling over for, or being a tool of, organized crime. Otherwise, legal gaming would never survive.

In July, 1958, Hank Greenspun, owner of the *Las Vegas Sun,* endorsed my candidacy in his "Where I Stand" column.

I had met him, and we had had a rather serious talk about the civil rights situation in the state. Although we disagreed on many things over the years, we totally agreed on that, and I believe that was the reason he supported me in the primary. Hank was friendly with Charlie Russell — as a great many people were — so I did not really expect his support in the general election, but he backed me all the way through.

George Franklin, one of my opponents in the primary, was at that point a Democrat. [laughter] (George was famous for switching. He was a Democrat two or three times; he was a Republican two or three times; and he ran for a lot offices — in fact, he once ran against McCarran. George was a colorful fellow.) Near the end of the primary I was in Eureka, where I got a telephone call from someone who told me George Franklin had put out fliers in the streets of Las Vegas and Reno that claimed I condoned prostitution. The fliers said there were five whorehouses operating in Elko County while I was district attorney; that children walked by them in the morning and at night when they went to school; and that I not only permitted this situation, but helped it to continue. I almost panicked when I received the call and had the flier read to me. I thought, "Oh, my God! This campaign is over; I'm done!"

Fortunately the press couldn't get to me in Eureka, and I had time to think things over. So the following day I issued a statement saying that "I am aware of the flier and its contents, which are unmitigated lies: in truth, there are *eight* houses of prostitution." I didn't attempt to answer any of the other charges, but that was the end of it. Everybody laughed, and the whole thing just went away.

During a campaign the candidate attempts to establish a theme that the public understands and ultimately either accepts or rejects, and I think that the public generally is able to separate the wheat from the chaff in the rhetoric. You will have your highs and lows, charges and counter charges, but the overall approach and personality of the candidate will come through, and he either wins or loses on that rather than on any specific charges . . . unless it's some sensational thing that the police get involved in, or you were found having sex with a sheep, or something like that. [laughter] That's why the charge that I was soft on prostitution was a laugh. And I got lucky in the way I responded: I didn't attempt to address the charge; therefore, the whole thing just became a joke. Besides, George Franklin was pretty well known to have a flair for bombast and for the extreme . . . perhaps too well known.

When I talked to my wife about running for state office, she made me promise that I would not spend any of our own money, which was an empty promise since we didn't have any. [laughter] But I never spent one penny in that campaign of what little money we did have. People began to send in small campaign donations even before I filed, and a few people were actually out working and soliciting donations — they weren't sure what I was going to run for, and neither was I, but they were raising money. The day I filed we had about seven thousand dollars ready for the primary campaign.

We figured that I could win narrowly in the primary if I could get 15 to 20 percent in Clark County, assuming we were right on the northern vote, which I figured to take by a large margin. As it turned out, I beat George Franklin in Clark County, and I think Harvey Dickerson beat me by a little, but not much. I got nearly a third of the vote in Clark, and the north came in about the way we expected it to . . . and I won the primary.[4] For me it was one of those extraordinary experiences that everybody should have an opportunity to enjoy at least once in a lifetime. You start out to try to do something with very little hope, and it gradually comes together in a way that you could never have imagined. Had I continued to run for office the rest of my life, I would never have had another experience that could possibly have compared to it: a group of well-intentioned amateurs, willing to sacrifice their own time and effort in a cause that they thought was proper . . . . (There was no comparison in the second campaign.) I think all of us who were involved feel that even if we were never a part of another extraordinary event, life had done us right by that primary victory.

Going in, we had all been indoctrinated pretty well with the idea that in Nevada an outsider running against an establishment person probably couldn't win . . . particularly an outsider coming from little Elko County. [laughter] George Franklin's candidacy hadn't tested that theory. He was sort of a loose cannon: colorful, interesting, and nobody knew how he would be received by the voters. But when I ran so well in Clark County against Harvey Dickerson, then I thought there was a reasonable chance that I could beat Charles Russell in the general election.

I didn't have much difficulty raising money for the general election, although we didn't spend a lot. It was a cheap campaign. Most people who support your campaign with money do it not because they think you are a terrific guy, but because they have some interest to protect, and they support you when they suddenly begin to think you have a chance to win. This may sound cynical, but I'm sure it is a fact. In Las Vegas I initially had little if any financial support, but after the rather shocking results of the primary, suddenly I had a lot of friends there, particularly on the Strip. It was obvious what had happened:

they had taken a look at the results and counted those votes and said, "You know, this guy might win. We better cover our bets and see if we can make a friend." They would need one, because in those days the governor totally controlled gaming. He appointed members of the Gaming Board, and members of the Gaming Commission served at his pleasure. He could fire them anytime he wanted — it was one-man control, and that made the governor by far the most important figure in the state for the gaming industry. Gaming people who before the primary wouldn't even speak to me (or anybody who went around on my behalf) suddenly began to show some interest.

In raising money from gaming, the general custom was for the candidate or somebody on the candidate's behalf to contact each of the major owners of casinos, as is still done today. They'd make an appointment and go by and talk to the person to see if he wanted to contribute. Bob McDonald was Alan Bible's man in Reno, the one who applied leverage to the local people for contributions, and he was a terrific fund raiser. He tells a story about my campaign:

Bob was raising money for Democratic candidates, and nobody knew me at all, so he called one of the local gamblers in Reno and said, "I've got a kid here running for governor that I want you to meet. I'll bring him by."

The guy said, "Don't bother; I don't want to meet him. Just drop by and pick up the money."

So Bob said to me, "I'm going to go get three thousand dollars for you." He went over and saw the guy who didn't want to be bothered, and brought back an envelope and said, "Here's your three thousand dollars."

Bob claims I counted it and said, "You're one hundred dollars short," and that I have been accusing him for the last thirty years of owing me one hundred dollars. [laughter]

There were no requirements at all for tracking donations in those days, and virtually all the contributions from the gaming community were in cash, so you had no way of knowing whether the money was from skim or coming out of profits. You had to go through the moral gymnastics of saying, "Now, this guy is offering me x thousand dollars from hotel y. Is it my responsibility to cross examine him as to where he got this money? Is it my responsibility to say to him, 'You've got to give it to me by check so that we can trace it'?" The answer to those questions — not only with me, but every other candidate — was no, it isn't! [laughter] And I didn't. We did have certain parameters, however. We kept very careful and detailed records of every penny that was contributed to my campaign. The records were not made public, because in those days you did not need to make them public, but for my own protection I wanted to have them. I had heard of instances in which people — either licensed or looking for a license — later had made claims that they had given very substantial sums to a candidate in cash, and I did not want to be in a position where I didn't know exactly what we had received from any specific person. And I would not accept contributions from any gaming people other than those licensed by the state, nor did I accept money from applicants or from people I had reason to believe would apply for a license.

Those who were acting on my behalf had to inform me of how much they received in campaign contributions, and from whom. My assumption was that they always turned in all the money, but I've since talked to office holders and candidates who claim that some acting for them did not always do that; they simply pocketed the money. Well, there's no protection against that, I guess, except to try to get people around you whom you trust. Most of the *major* contributions would go directly to the candidate, but there were always a lot of smaller sums coming in through other people, and you just had to assume that those were going to be accounted for.

I didn't know Governor Russell well, but I had the feeling that it was time for a change, time for a new look and new energy, and that was the theme of my campaign. My literature featured a photograph of me striding forward, one foot boldly out in front of the other, a glow all around me. [laughter] I had a crew cut. That projected the image of a young man on the move — vigorous, in contrast to what we were alleging to be an administration that was asleep at the switch and not doing anything. I don't know how effective campaign literature and posters and any of those things are by themselves, but if they are part of a theme, and if they're good enough, they'll add to the campaign's impetus. I was happy with ours.

In northern Nevada the feeling of hostility toward Clark County was probably even more intense than it is now, but my strategy for the general election was the reverse of what it had been in the primary campaign: in the general I thought I could probably carry Clark County, which was heavily Democratic in those days. Like me, Charlie Russell, the incumbent governor, was from the north, from Ely, so my effort became to try to stay even with him in upstate, and let Clark carry me to victory. However, as the campaign got underway the perception started to emerge in the north that I was their candidate, and I began to feel that I could attract some Republican votes there that would normally not go to a Democrat. So I had to get organized in the south and try to hold the organizations that I had in the north. We attempted to organize every county, and had campaign chairmen in each, but I concentrated most of my efforts in Las Vegas. With more money coming in for the general election than had come in for the primary, we could be a little bit more flexible in what we did. My goal was to increase interest in my candidacy among as many groups as I could, and build what I hadn't really been able to build in the primary.

Whoever said it was to my advantage that nobody knew me in Las Vegas was right. I was something different after eight years of Charlie's picture in the paper every day. There was a perception among the voters that he was just a laid-back kind of guy, and during the campaign I played on that by portraying his administration as "do-nothing." I tended to overstate and over-dramatize this, but the fact is that he did have that reputation: "Do nothing unless you have to." His whole administration sort of had that image: "We won't take any initiatives; we'll just ride with the tide and hope for the best."

My campaign rhetoric notwithstanding, nobody who knew Charlie Russell could have been critical of him as a person. He was an honorable fellow who always did his best, and I think he will go down as a very good governor. But after eight years in office everybody has made some enemies, and you don't make many new friends being governor — each day brings new animosities if you are doing anything at all. As I got to know him better I came to the conclusion that Charlie Russell was a man of real principle and considerable ability. Despite my criticism of him during the height of the campaign, the record will show that he was a good governor. I look back on him with admiration for a man who served his state well.

I didn't expect a big victory, but near the end I thought I was at least going to win, because in the last six weeks we saw things happening in Clark County — things began to come together. Even so, I was unprepared for the eventual margin. By a substantial majority, I had been elected governor of Nevada.[5] My elation was short-lived.

Part Two

governor of nevada,
1959-1966

5

---

a turbulent start

My first year in office was stormy, and I never want to go through another year like it. Right after the election some of my people and I traveled to Death Valley, and for three or four days we just sat and discussed Nevada's problems and what we wanted to do about them. We also talked over some of my proposed administrative appointments. After that meeting at Death Valley, I started sitting down with key people in state government, many of them Russell appointees. Since I wasn't particularly knowledgeable about either state government or the people who were in it, I was really kind of groping at that point, and a lot was instinct. Shortly it was reported in the press that I expected key department heads in the previous administration to submit their resignations when I took office. This was controversial, to say the least. Some of the press voiced concern; some of the public were upset; and some of the bureaucrats in Carson City were *terribly* distressed. My feeling was that if we were going to have a new deal, we ought to have a new deal! And anyway, I hadn't said that I was going to replace everybody, but that I should have the option of appointing people.

Almost immediately after assuming office I became embroiled in a dispute over my executive authority to dismiss bureaucrats. In any administration people in key positions must be willing to accept new policies and directions, and to be loyal, but Charles Oliver, director of the Drivers' License Division, was by no stretch of the imagination on the Sawyer team. He was a person that you couldn't even talk to without his calling a press conference the same day to report some things that were true, some things that were not. I requested that he submit his resignation, and as counsel he retained Paul Laxalt, who told him not to do it. (At the same time Laxalt was under pressure to resign from the Nevada Industrial Commission because of his highly partisan Republican politics.)

Mr. Oliver was just one of a number of bureaucrats I inherited who were very fond of Governor Russell, were not fond of me at all, and were not about to change their attitudes. Some of these folks had civil service protection, and a few were classified employees of the state. They couldn't be removed except for cause, and when I asked them to submit their resignations, most of them refused to do so. So for years I was saddled with leaders in some major departments who were antagonistic toward the administration that they were supposed to be a part of. It was a frustrating and exhausting experience for me, at least in the beginning. You just can't operate a state government that way, and as Russell's appointees filled out whatever was left of their terms, I replaced most of them; but I kept some on, because although it was my obligation to change things, that didn't mean I should run willy-nilly over good people in government. I did appoint replacements for the many people who had just gotten too comfortable in their jobs. After all, Charlie Russell had been governor for eight years . . . .

Governor Russell was very kind to me between the election and my inauguration. He gave me an office in the state capitol, and I sat in that office and people streamed through all day, every day, many of them demanding jobs. I was so naive that I had believed everybody was supporting me because they thought I would make a good governor, but I was shocked to learn how many felt that if I were elected I would do something for them . . . unfortunately, that's the way it was. I was surprised to discover that the greatest number of people wanted to be appointed to the Nevada Boxing Commission. Members of the commission sit ringside, and they get to travel all over the world. They are also announced before fights, and they have a lot of meetings and fame. It's a wonderful appointment. The next in demand was a seat on the State Gaming Commission.

Most appointive government positions are filled through a combination of patronage and qualifications, and you're certainly not going to sacrifice your own reputation and effectiveness by appointing a political hack to an important job. If you have a person who was part of your team when you were running, and is qualified to do a good job, that's a nice combination. If, however, you start to fill important jobs with just political people who have no skill, then that's self-defeating. It's bad government. But the moment I was elected, forty people were claiming that they were totally responsible for my election and that I owed them something. Some of these were people I'd never heard of, but they were relentless. Talking to Bruce Barnum about one of them, I said, "This lady has called me repeatedly, written letters and everything else, demanding to be appointed to something. She claims that she carried a whole precinct for me, and I don't know who she is. We've got to do something to get her off my back! Is there any appointment I can give her where she can't do any damage?"

Bruce looked down the list and he finally said, "Well, there's an appointment here on the Indian Commission."

I said, "For God's sake, appoint her!" [laughter]

That was pure patronage; I don't think that woman had the slightest qualification to be on the Indian Commission. To be honest, there are some people that you just do those things for, and try to put them where they can't do any damage, and the Indian Commission had virtually no power.

My lieutenant governor was Rex Bell, a Republican. Given the difference in party, we had about as good a relationship as we could have had, and Bette and I liked him very much. Rex was perfectly honorable and trustworthy, and when I talked with him about matters involving state government I never feared any double dealing or partisanship. I included him in all the functions at the mansion — he told me that until I was elected he hadn't been in it, even though he had served under a Republican. (I think it was because of his marital status. Apparently there was some concern that his wife wasn't with him, but that was of no concern at all to us.)

Nevada's lieutenant governors are elected on their own rather than as part of the gubernatorial ticket. Thus, in each of my terms I wound up with a Republican lieutenant governor — Rex Bell in the first and Paul Laxalt in the second — and we didn't have the team unity which would have been possible if lieutenant governors were elected on the same ticket . . . which I have always felt would be a good idea. In similar contrast with federal practice, Nevada's cabinet officers are popularly elected rather than appointed, and they are not answerable to the governor. I might have liked and respected these men, but their constituencies, political agendas, and partisan interests were different from mine, so they were not, as a rule, part of my kitchen cabinet. Now, I did have John Koontz, who was secretary of state. He was a good old Democrat who wasn't necessarily a Sawyer person, but we had very cordial relations. I also had cordial relations with Roger Foley, who was attorney general, but Roger had his own political agenda, which wasn't necessarily the same as mine. So I tended to go outside the elected cabinet and consult with my own people.

Bruce Barnum was the person I chose as my executive assistant. No matter what that position is called, every governor has had somebody in his office to handle administrative matters and ride herd on the staff. Each member of my staff had some specific duty that he or she was responsible for, and obviously I was not going to run around every morning to check on whether or not the extradition secretary (for example) was doing his job. So you have to have a sort of chief of staff, and in the first several years Bruce was the person who coordinated activities in the office and between department heads. He would receive complaints — and we had many of them — about various departments and individuals in government, and he would attempt to resolve those problems, whatever they were. Bruce also handled much of my correspondence, even though it came in to be signed by me. If, for example, we got an inquiry about water, he would see that the state engineer received that inquiry and supplied an answer, which he would then put in letter form for me. I would look at it and sign it, and it would be sent out.

The duties of the executive assistant are myriad, and you have to be able to trust him totally, because a lot of confidential things go on, and a great many confidential communications come in to a governor. And a governor can't deal with the many relatively small problems that are sent his way, so the executive assistant handles them too. He has to know what you are thinking, and he's got to be able to come to you with solutions, not problems. Then if you accept those solutions, he steps in and does whatever needs to be done.

I was an advocate of going to annual legislative sessions, with even-numbered years limited to fiscal and economic matters. The legislature supported the proposal, which then went on the ballot.[1] After the public approved it, there was one infamous annual session — just one, in 1960. Not satisfied with being restricted to things fiscal, the legislators broadened their interpretation of the law until they had what amounted to a regular session, staying in Carson City for God knows how long and passing every bill in the book. The public and I were so disgusted with this butchery that they soon repealed the law, and there never has been another scheduled annual session . . . which may be unfortunate. I still think that had they followed my suggestion and limited each even-numbered session to thirty days, permitting consideration of only a narrow range of fiscal and economic matters, it would have been beneficial. We need it now even more than we did then.

There was a lot of innate rivalry between the legislative and executive branches, and the legislature historically was very tight when it came to the budget for the governor's office — they made sure that he didn't have too much help floating around, and both the office and the mansion were bare-bones operations. In fact, when we moved into the mansion it contained no furniture! [laughter] Up until my election, I guess every governor had been rich and had a big house, and brought his own furniture (believe it or not) and put it in the mansion. But we had nothing. We had enough furniture to fill one little anteroom, and that was it; the rest of the mansion was empty. Governor Russell moved all of his furniture out, and suddenly Nevada had a poor governor who couldn't furnish the official residence . . . incredible, but true.

We had a hell of a time convincing the legislature that they had to do something to get us some furniture. I mean, if they wanted to come over for a cocktail party, they had to have something to sit on. We even used our own table settings, such as they were, for a long time . . . until they all got stolen. Whenever we had a party, knives and forks would be gone, plates taken . . . unbelievable! And it was ours. People didn't realize that it was not state property, but our property. Of course, the theft continued even after we got state-paid-for property.

Initially, about the only things we had in the mansion were the few pieces of furniture we brought from Elko, and a large dining room table and some chairs. That was it; there was nothing else. So Bette invited over the chairman of the ways and means committee and the chairman of the senate finance committee, and she showed them around. She said, "Now, look: we can survive this all right; we've got the same furniture we had before we came here. But if you expect the legislature to come over for a cocktail party, or dinner, or whatever, we have to have an appropriation for some furniture."

In addition, Nevada would be hosting the Winter Olympics in 1960, and we were looking at entertaining the whole International Olympic Committee, and royalty from all over Europe, and members of parliament from England, and so on . . . with no furniture. It was just shameful. Maude Frazier[2] became very active in raising money to furnish the mansion, and, as I remember, we got some barely in time to entertain those folks. And finally we got a legislative appropriation that was fairly substantial for those days. Bette then dealt with various purveyors of china, furniture, and so on, and some art was donated to us, and the place was made presentable.

The pace and schedule needed to run the state government were exhausting, and I would drastically change my style if I were ever governor again. (Which will never happen!) You have to remember that during my years as governor the population of Nevada was still relatively small. If there was a civic organization meeting in Elko, I would get a call from somebody saying, "I'm your biggest supporter here, and I promised them that I would get you to come to the meeting."

That's a rather difficult thing to handle. You say, "Elko is three hundred miles away. How can I get there? I don't have the time."

They reply, "But you owe us."

I felt sort of an obligation to try to accommodate those kinds of requests. As I look back on it now, and my wife and I have discussed this many times, I just should have said no.

In comparing my activities of that kind with governors of New York, California, New Jersey, and Pennsylvania, I found that I was doing ten times as much of that as they were in their larger states. I finally concluded that the larger the state, the fewer personal appearances are required. Elsewhere they don't expect you to attend the American Legion meeting, but in Nevada they do because you're their friend. They were for you, and you know them, and you went to school with their cousin — but that doesn't happen in California and in New York. Governor Nelson Rockefeller told me he was making only two or three public appearances a month, while I would attend at least one public function every day. Doing this also exposes you to public criticism because you're supposed to be in Carson City tending to the affairs of state, not running all over to speak to every group of more than three people. In short, I think I made a mistake in doing as much as I did. Fortunately, I was young and I was in good physical condition.

Richard Bryan, I would say, was almost as frantic as I was when he was governor. There have been other Nevada governors, though, who were much more laid back and didn't make so many appearances . . . they took vacations and that sort of thing, which was totally foreign to me. But I think they were right and I was wrong. From my perspective now, those things did not do me one bit of political good; I don't think they made the slightest bit of difference.

I also traveled a great deal trying to attract business into the state for economic diversification, going to places throughout the country to promote the advantages of Nevada's climate and tax policy. This idea originated with an organization in Las Vegas called SNIF, the Southern Nevada Industrial Foundation, predecessor to our present organization for economic development. As governor I agreed to accompany SNIF's officers on some of the recruiting visits they were making. We would have a cocktail party and invite whoever we could, trying to get press coverage of our little speeches about how great Nevada was, and so on.

Nevada had something called the Freeport Act,[3] and that was a big talking point when we traveled out of state. It attracted quite a lot of industry, particularly warehousing, to northern Nevada, but not too much to the south. Warehousers could bring their goods into the state, store and reassemble them, and then ship the goods out with no tax, and there were just one or two other states that permitted that. Even though you were giving up what you could otherwise have taxed, at least you were bringing people and industry into the state.

My travel in the interests of economic diversification was different from anything that had been done before, and it became politically controversial and the subject of press ridicule. It was kind of ironic: I was doing a good job of selling Nevada, but they didn't want me to go anyplace to sell it. [laughter] The "gallivantin' Grant" moniker that they pinned on me was like what they did to Bryan McKay in his last term as attorney general when they started publishing a chart of the mileage he was racking up on out-of-state travel . . . but my trips were more focused, in that they were aimed specifically at spreading the good word about Nevada. Many of the places I visited were places you would rather not be, so I wasn't out having a gas every time I took a trip. It's easy to stay in Carson City for eight years, but it isn't always easy to get out and hustle, which is what we were doing.

I'm not as enthusiastic about growth and development as I once was, but that was a whole different time and a different place; and in truth I was as concerned about Nevada's image as I was about growth. I thought if we visited other places in the country and showed them that we were something other than a bunch of people who had just come out from behind the crap table, that might change our image. While trying to attract a wider spectrum of people and industries to the state, I didn't criticize gaming; but I felt that a broader base would not only help us economically, it would help us image-wise: "These Nevadans are the same as any other people."

My first year in office was a terrible ordeal, and in some respects the situation did not improve in succeeding years. On June 23, 1961, I was

"No, I'm Not Taking Any Trips"

arrested for violating the open meeting law which the legislature had just passed — so was the attorney general. Open-meeting laws were big in those days. The press was saying, "Let the press in," and it was sponsoring open-meeting laws all around the country. It's difficult for legislators to say no when the press says, "We want you to support this open-meeting law so we don't have any more secret meetings. The public is entitled to know all of this." They've got to run again in a short period of time, when they hope to have the support of the press. So the press really pushed this and put the arm on enough legislators to pass the law, and I didn't object to it or resist. I signed it.

A short time later Attorney General Roger Foley, Controller Keith Lee, and I were in the governor's office discussing some highway problems. (We were on the Highway Board by statute.) We were sitting there having a quiet meeting, when in marched a gendarme of some kind from the district court across the street. We were allegedly violating the law that I had just signed a few days before! A complaint had been filed by the *Reno Gazette* reporter who covered the political scene in Carson City, charging us with a crime. So all three of us were arrested and taken across the street to the court. (The *Gazette* was a Republican newspaper in those years, and we were all Democrats. This fact did not escape me.) Needless to say, that was a hell of a story. [laughter] I was just getting ready to go to a national governors' conference, and this hit the newspapers all over the country: Nevada's governor, attorney general, and controller had all been arrested. At the conference every governor knew all about it, and everybody was saying, "Well, what did you do? What heinous crime did you commit?"

To represent them in this big criminal matter, Foley and Lee hired Bert Goldwater and George Vargas, who was a big Republican in Nevada and had the largest law firm in Reno, and I think I hired the Bill Woodburn firm to represent me. A motion to dismiss was filed, the motion was granted, and that was the end of that. It had never occurred to any of us that we were holding a secret meeting. We'd been doing this all the time with all of our statutory boards and commissions, and everybody who had preceded us had done the same thing for years.

To the reporter who provoked this incident by filing the complaint, I said, "Do you realize what you've done to us by this act? For the rest of our lives when we fill out job application forms, or anything else, and we come to the question, 'Have you ever been arrested for a crime? Yes; Convicted? No; If not, please explain . . . .'" And that turned out to be the case. When Roger Foley was being considered for federal judge he told me that that arrest gave him a lot of problems, and I also ran into it in forms that I had to fill out. Insofar as the *Gazette* was concerned, before it was over the affair was an embarrassment to them, too. It was really too much!

Nothing, however, was as controversial in Nevada as travel by the governor, and I was often out of state. In April, 1962, I made a tour of Japan with several other governors. Put together by the National Governors' Conference, the trip was partially funded by the state department. There wasn't much in it for Nevada, although you could say that the Pacific Rim was important to us in terms of tourism and industry, and any exposure that the state got in that area might be productive. We traveled to every state in Japan, visiting schools and the respective mayors and governors in all the areas as a good-will, hands-across-the-sea gesture, similar to a trip that we later took to South America.

President Kennedy had asked me to give an address in Hiroshima, the purpose of my speech being to try to ameliorate the terribly hard feelings toward America caused by our dropping the atomic bomb. I spoke in front of the Hiroshima monument, which was erected in remembrance of the people who had died in that bombing. Relatives and friends of the victims attended the ceremony, and it was a very difficult speech to give, because we were not there to open up old wounds. To try to explain to those people the rationale behind the nuclear death of their relatives and friends and thousands of other people killed when the bomb dropped was not easy.

Not too long after that trip, Japan's governors' association decided to come to America, and one of the places they visited was Las Vegas. We had quite a riotous time with the Japanese, many of whom had never been to the United States, particularly to a place like Las Vegas! We were trying to keep this a relatively formal state occasion, and they were always sneaking off to see the naked women in the girlie shows. [laughter] It was really quite funny. Wherever there was anything interesting going on (particularly if it was sexually oriented), they were very eager. So we herded them around for several days, and when they left we were just exhausted from trying to keep everything on a high level.

In June, 1962, there was a change in my staff. Bruce Barnum and Dick Ham switched jobs. Mr. Barnum was a competent man, a close friend of mine, and he really got the better of the deal in the switch we made, taking over a much larger organization that was federally funded: he became the Employment Security Director. But at the time we were thinking seriously about reelection . . . and Dick was from Clark County, where most of the voters were, while Bruce was not. It seemed wise to have someone in the governor's immediate family from Las Vegas; and after weighing all the considerations, I felt that my executive assistant should be more connected with Clark County than Bruce was.

Neither Bruce nor Dick seemed to be upset by the change in their assignments, and Bruce was probably happy to get out from under all the tension, strain, and stress of being the front man in the governor's office. The position that he assumed was much more comfortable because it wasn't nearly as high profile media-wise. It also commanded a higher salary. On the other hand, Dick Ham was an activist with a political background who was quite aggressive, and I think he welcomed the challenge in his new job.

Another person who got a new job was Assemblywoman Maude Frazier. There had never been a woman lieutenant governor in the state of Nevada, but in 1962, when Rex Bell died in office, I appointed Maude to fill the vacancy. Maude had had a long, distinguished career as an educator in Las Vegas, and she was a legislator of total conviction who could not be cowed, swayed, or leveraged by anybody . . . and contrary to some of the criticism, she still possessed all of her faculties despite her age, believe me! I admired her virtues, and believed that by experience she was as qualified as anybody in the state to assume the office of lieutenant governor. I also thought the appointment would be a cap-stone to her career, and a reward for her long public service. It was a pleasure to appoint her, and I didn't really care what anybody said.

6

---

getting gaming
under control

Governor Russell had created a Gaming Control Board to monitor adherence to gambling regulations in Nevada, but under his plan the Tax Commission continued as the body with the final say.[1] When I took office I wanted gaming control to be strengthened; and with the support of some legislators (from both parties, as I remember), I proposed that the Tax Commission should henceforth be dedicated exclusively to tax matters, and replaced as gaming regulator by a state gaming commission, with the Gaming Control Board given the responsibility for enforcing the gaming laws. In January, 1959, in my first state-of-the-state message, I recommended my new regulation system. Although there was some opposition, no partisan dispute developed, and the proposal was enacted into law.[2]

As the enforcement wing of the commission, the Gaming Control Board had (and has) all the staff; the commission, none. The board's three members were and are appointed by the governor, as are the members of the commission, and they can only be removed for cause, although they originally served at the pleasure of the governor. Qualifications for appointment to the commission and board are left to the judgment of the governor, with the exception of some statutory requirements. For example, you need one person on the board with an accounting background to deal with money questions: Where does the money come from? Where does the money go? Is it all being accounted for? Is there any skim? The expertise to explore these questions is essential. You will also find a law enforcement person on the board, and there will be a member with general administrative experience and ability.

For my appointees to both the commission and the board I went with people who had a high profile in law enforcement . . . and people who were familiar with gaming and shared my belief that its control was dismally inadequate in Nevada. It made no difference to me whether they were Republican or Democrat, but they had to be people who could command respect on the national level as well as the state, because our relations with federal authorities were not good. In appointing members to the board or commission, I looked for integrity. Can this person be trusted? There are so many ways that members can be gotten to, and not just with money. You had to be sure that your appointees were incorruptible: that they would not take advantage of their positions financially or otherwise; that they wouldn't even take free tickets to a ball game. I wouldn't put any of my friends on the commission or the board, either . . . they didn't have the qualifications, and in addition to that, I know my friends, and that is the last place I would want some of them! [laughter] And I didn't appoint anybody to the commission from the gaming industry, which was a matter of some concern to them. But at that time there was a lot of rumor and gossip about crime and corruption in Nevada gaming — it was a national issue (there had even been congressional hearings on it), and I felt that members had to be above any possible reproach.

I was in a vulnerable position. If I made a mistake in my appointments my whole career would be on the line, because appointments are made by the governor alone. The senate has always wanted an advice and consent role regarding gaming control, but they've never gotten it; and I wouldn't favor it even now, because to be an effective executive you have to decide who is going to be on the boat and who is going to be running it. A bunch of people who meet every two years, coming up with their buddies and their favorites . . . that can't make for a very good operation.

By and large I was pleased with my appointees. There may have been one or two little problems, but nothing of any consequence. I didn't reappoint one member when his term expired — not that it was anything serious: it was just one of those situations where a person who never had much authority suddenly was invested with tremendous power, and really couldn't handle it, and became greatly impressed with his position. That happened not just in gaming, but in some other appointments that I made. People would just change overnight from the person you thought you knew, and would become a different personality . . . that just happens with some people.

Our approach to gaming regulation has worked out reasonably well, although there is a spirit of competition between the Gaming Control Board (which is the investigative and regulatory body), and the Gaming Commission, which often does not follow the recommendations of the board.

Board positions are full-time, whereas the commissioners are part-time, so sometimes the board feels as though the commissioners are a bunch of amateurs who don't understand — egos are sometimes wounded when the commission overturns the board's recommendations. But I am not sure that this built-in rivalry is all bad, because every applicant gets a double shot: once when the board makes recommendations to the commission, and again when the final action is taken. Throughout the world (including new Jersey) our system has served as a model for most jurisdictions that have legalized casino gaming.

Back when I was governor we were dealing with a different breed in gaming than we have today. Many in the industry were alleged to have come from unsavory backgrounds, from the mob as it were, and they were experts at applying leverage and exerting undue influence — if not with money, then by other means, such as catching you in a compromising position. As governor I had to be constantly aware of this, to the point that I almost had to have a protector around me all the time. I couldn't even stay in a hotel room by myself! I had to have people around me who could not be gotten to, and I selected only men whom I knew well or who came to me with very strong recommendations.

There were always stories being written about corruption in Nevada. In 1960 *Life* magazine came out with an article saying the mob had tried to buy our state government in 1958 when Charlie Russell was governor. In those days we were getting that kind of story all the time . . . just one exposé after another, like the book *The Green Felt Jungle*. After a while it began to get to me. You consider yourself an honorable person surrounded by honorable people, and to be

RECORD TIME

Throwing The Book at Them

Las Vegas Review-Journal 2/15/62

constantly accused of being something less gets to be very annoying. I developed the attitude, "By God, I will show these people that Nevadans are like everybody else, with the same principles and the same standards — maybe better than some other people. We are not the riffraff that they make us out to be, nor are we for sale to anybody!"

In my inaugural address to the legislature I said that it was the policy of my administration that we would not tolerate any organized crime influence in Nevada, and I invited the FBI to tell us if they knew of any mob presence in the state. Although I questioned the alleged extent of mob influence, I wasn't so dumb that I didn't realize that some of the licensees came out of organized criminal backgrounds. There wasn't really anything I could do about those who were already here and licensed before I was elected except watch them carefully; but when a new applicant for a gaming license came along, one of our first inquiries would be to the FBI to see if they had a rap sheet[3] on that person (they would always provide us with a copy if they did), and during my eight years as governor I don't believe we licensed anybody who later turned out to have ties with organized crime. Ultimately, all the people who were suspected died off or left the state, so there's virtually no organized criminal activity in gaming in Nevada now.

When I took office Nevada had recently experienced the embarrassment of the Kefauver hearings, which created a national sensation, so we took rather forceful measures to address our problem. I think it was the press that called my gaming policy the "hang tough" policy, taking the term out of the first address I gave to the legislature. I had just appointed the new gaming board and commission, and in my speech I encouraged them to hang tough. I said that the feds had accused us of harboring organized crime figures in Nevada, and that if they were here we should find them and get them out. That was the whole tenor of the speech. The press had to call it something, so they called it the "hang tough" policy.

I got constant complaints from licensees about the aggressiveness of the Control Board, but I had already established my position on that: unless the agents were completely out of line and doing something illegal, then I wanted them to be aggressive and forceful . . . and I wanted this known to the national press, to Congress, and to the attorney general of the United States. This was all part of what I hoped would be a change in the image of our control of gambling. I wanted the state perceived as a clean, progressive, and tough enforcer of the law, and I assumed that most people (with the possible exception of some owners of gaming establishments) would applaud our efforts to clean up this state if it needed to be cleaned up . . . but political life is full of surprises.

In December of 1960, Attorney General Roger B. Foley blasted me in the press for my "hang tough" policy, which he characterized as gestapo tactics. The chairman of the Gaming Commission was former FBI agent Milt Keefer, who lives in Las Vegas to this day. He had ordered the surveillance of casinos down on the Strip in an effort to determine if they were being entered by any of the undesirables listed in Nevada's "black book." Ray Abbaticchio, chairman of the Gaming Control Board, was responsible for enforcing the black book, and his activities prompted Attorney General Foley to publicly attack the methods of the board.

"Black book" was a term that was coined by the press. (It was officially called the *List of Excluded Persons*.) The black book originated when people I had appointed to the Gaming Control Board and the Gaming Commission came to me and said, "We would like to create a list of known unsavory people who frequent hotels and casinos in Nevada. Many of these people are alleged to be involved with the mob, and they have a good deal to do with all of the bad publicity that we are getting about organized criminals associating with owners of casinos." They felt that the list should not be secret — that it should be published, so that when they complained to an owner that his place was frequented by organized crime figures, he wouldn't be able to say, "I didn't know that Sam Giancana was connected with the mob when I hosted him, comped his room, and comped all his meals." [laughter]

In theory I thought they had a good idea, but perhaps one that was unconstitutional. I didn't see how we could put somebody's name on a list and say, "You can't go into a public accommodation." But they thought differently, and because I was in favor of doing anything within the law to keep those people out of Nevada, I authorized them to go ahead. Not long after the black book came out Johnny Marshall, one of the fellows listed in it, was discovered in the Desert Inn. The Desert Inn was asked to eject him, and he wound up suing me and the state of Nevada, and I guess members of the Gaming Control Board and Gaming Commission. Somewhat to my surprise the courts held that we had the right to have him ejected, and the Ninth Circuit Court sustained that ruling! [laughter] I always had the feeling that on a purely civil rights basis we were extending ourselves, but the courts have consistently affirmed the constitutionality of our approach.[4]

The black book worked to a certain extent, although we could never make the list long enough! [laughter] Consistent with what I kept saying we were all about, it served notice that we were trying to do something about getting organized crime out of the gaming industry. It's a tool that's still used, but since those early days they have added a lot of protection for the poor soul who is about to go on the list: he is entitled to notice and to a hearing, neither of which applied initially. These protections were added by Nevada officials over the years in fairness, and I fully support them. A person now has a chance to vindicate himself and show that he shouldn't be in there before his name is entered.

With the black book, we were dealing with the tension between the police powers of the state and traditional first and fourteenth amendment guarantees of individual rights. Those are difficult issues. Excluding individuals from all areas of a casino — prohibiting them from dining there, swimming there, or in any way being inside, even if it's for a political function — may be going a bit far. On the other hand, there is the obligation of the state to protect the health and welfare of its citizens and its industry. The federal courts have distinguished between the generic idea of public accommodations for everybody and for certain special classes. In this case, there was a special class (criminals and their associates) which had been named in the black book.[5] Courts held that the duty of the state to protect the welfare of its citizens took priority in this particular case over the rights of those few people who were listed in the black book.

There may very well have been some mob influence during my years in office; but if there were, I certainly didn't have any specifics, and I am confident that the people in charge of enforcement and control of gaming couldn't find any . . . and the federal agencies that were claiming mob influence would not give us any information that we could act on. In fact, the FBI and the Justice Department gave us no help at all. Our first move in that direction was to try to establish communications with the FBI, and our gaming people met with them and talked with them and worked up what we thought was a mutually beneficial exchange of information. It didn't take very long before we realized that it was a one-way street — we were advising them of everything that we knew, and we were getting nothing in return. That became evident when, after a meeting, we would read in the newspaper about something that the FBI knew about but had not discussed with us.

In this attempt at collaboration I was saddled with J. Edgar Hoover, who was obviously using everything to his own advantage — he would take the bows for any information we gave him, as if it were newly discovered on his part. A man of tremendous ego, Hoover wanted credit for everything, often to the disadvantage and surprise of our state. And it just wouldn't work. He was running rampant over federal and state laws in his activities, and he posed a terrible threat not just to Nevada, but to America in general. I was not shy about telling people that some way or another he ought to be curtailed, but I found little support for taking action . . . . I even went to the president of the United States about him. It was generally known in those days that J. Edgar Hoover had dossiers on all key congressional people, senators, and certainly presidents and vice-presidents. These people naturally were very concerned, because they didn't know what was in the dossiers, and they were afraid to challenge Hoover. Ultimately we had to take a new tack: we stopped talking to the FBI. No more one-way street.

In the summer of 1961 Roger Foley learned of a federal strike force that was being put together to invade every major casino in Reno and Las Vegas — the Department of Justice asked him to deputize sixty-five federal agents to carry out this big raid on Nevada gambling. I was stunned. The day after Roger told me, we got on a plane and went to Washington and I made an appointment to see the attorney general. To my recollection it was on a weekend, because when I was shown in to see Bobby Kennedy I found him dressed for a game of tennis or something. I asked if he was planning to raid Nevada; and if so, why? We had a heated discussion, to say the least, and there was no give or compromise on his part at all. He looked at Nevada, as many people then did, as a den of iniquity . . . everybody who lived in or came to Nevada was corrupt, including me, and to clean the state up he was ready to assign a substantial force of agents to raid it. I took great exception to that, because we had a pretty effective enforcement policy in Nevada by that time. And apart from everything else, Bobby's plan made no political sense: the last time I had seen him before this was in Los Angeles at the 1960 Democratic convention, when he came to my room pleading for the Nevada votes for his brother.

We had tried desperately to cooperate with the FBI in an exchange of information, and we had offered numerous times to clean up anything that the attorney general, his staff, or the FBI felt was going on — if they would simply tell us, we would take care of it. But here in the middle of what we thought was a cooperative effort to deal jointly with our problems, I discovered this secret plan. The media sensationalizing that would attend such a federal raid could do our state great damage, and I was shocked that neither the Nevada attorney general nor myself had been extended the courtesy of being informed. There were already more federal agents per capita in Nevada than any place in the world [laughter], and I suspected that the planned invasion in force was a publicity stunt as much as anything else. Bobby Kennedy wanted to show the people of the United States that he was the guy to clean up all sin and corruption, and Nevada was a great place to start.

You had to experience the attitude of Easterners concerning Nevada . . . . It was then almost endemic in the bureaucracy and the Washington establishment, and we are seeing it now with the nuclear dump issue when senators and congressmen refer to Nevada as a wasteland. It was that attitude that Bobby Kennedy projected: "You are a bunch of peasants out there; you're all sort of sleazy. We here in the East, who know all, are going to come out there and set you right, whether you like it or not." As a personal matter I was particularly offended, because I got the impression that Bobby looked upon me as someone who had just stepped out from behind a crap table; and he seemed to imply that I was connected with the mob, which really burned me up. I remember pounding the table and just feeling that I was making no progress with him at all.

The day after my confrontation with Bobby I went up to the White House. I had not gone to Washington intending to see the president, but after receiving no satisfaction from Bobby I felt it was necessary, and Jack Kennedy and I met alone in the Oval Office. As I told him the story and described the devastating effect I thought this raid would have on Nevada, I got the impression that he knew nothing about his brother's plan. I explained the progress we were making in the state with respect to enforcement and control, and said that I thought the planned action was a precipitous move on the part of his attorney general. Not only would it be terribly damaging to Nevada, it would accomplish little in the national context. The president was very cordial, very nice. He made no commitments, but the raid never occurred.

Had the raid ever come off, the political consequences for me would have been pretty devastating, and I was very aware of that. I felt personally betrayed, because I had given my support to the president and tried to convince everybody in Nevada that he was a great guy and that he would be sensitive to our problems and all of that; then to have his administration turn on us almost immediately after the election was a bit of political treachery. And I was concerned that the planned action would be damaging to our congressional delegation. Though they had not supported Kennedy at the convention (Senators Bible and Cannon supported Lyndon Johnson), it would have been political disaster for them if all of us combined did not command enough respect from the Democratic administration to stop this cheap, sensational move on the part of the attorney general . . . if we couldn't do that, we didn't amount to much. I conveyed that to the president, and he understood my point.

Even after my meeting with President Kennedy, although the raid was cancelled, the general situation in Nevada improved very little. In 1963, Carl Cohen, a 10 percent shareholder in the Sands, found microphones in his office, and I believe in his house, and other top-ranking casino executives in this state were wire-tapped. This was disgraceful. If you have a federal law, you should abide by it everywhere, not just everywhere but Nevada! We also had state laws that prohibited that kind of eavesdropping without court sanction.

In November that year I wrote to Attorney General Kennedy and enclosed some of the news clippings of the wiretapping . . . in essence I was asking what was going on. My impression was that none of these wiretaps had been sanctioned under federal law; I doubt that any court had ordered them or endorsed them, and I took the position publicly that Bobby Kennedy and J. Edgar Hoover were violating federal and state law. I'm sure I was right, but *nobody* dared move against J. Edgar Hoover in those days; and although he and Bobby Kennedy were not friends, Kennedy would do nothing to restrain Hoover and his FBI. Between the two of them, they were trampling on the constitutional right to privacy of the citizens of this country.

My relationship with Bobby Kennedy never improved. I hadn't particularly cared for him before this incident — his arrogance and his cavalier attitude turned me off even during

Frank Sinatra entertains Marilyn Monroe at his Cal-Neva Lodge, 1959. *"Because he was Sinatra, it was obvious that we would have a problem enforcing regulations . . . . I told Ed Olsen, 'Do not be intimidated by him.'"*

the 1960 campaign — and after our confrontation I had no use for him at all. I didn't trust him, and I didn't support him later when he decided to run for president . . . I wouldn't have supported him under any conditions, even if it meant I had to support a Republican instead. [laughter] The thought that Bobby might become president of the United States was frightening. Anyone who would use and manipulate a federal agency the way he was attempting to was dangerous, and I put him in the same category as J. Edgar Hoover.

Sam Giancana, subpoenaed by a Chicago federal grand jury investigating organized crime, disappeared in the summer of 1963. It was later discovered that he was staying at Frank Sinatra's Cal-Neva Lodge at Lake Tahoe. Giancana was a hoodlum of national repute who was listed in the black book, and there was no question that the Cal-Neva was violating Nevada gaming regulations, but when officials of the Gaming Control Board launched an investigation, Sinatra bullied, badgered and harassed them. He was so rude to the Gaming Control agents that it was almost unbelievable. I read a telephone transcript in which he used every filthy word in the book . . . arrogant, threatening language! He dished out astonishing abuse — who were we in Nevada to question *him?* [Appended to this book the reader will find a more detailed account of this incident as recalled by Ed Olsen, chairman of the Nevada Gaming Control Board at the time.] Of course, Sinatra's a very abusive guy under any circumstances. My experience with him has been that he sets his own rules; he does his own thing, regardless, and he has violated laws with impunity and bought his way out of most problems if he could.

Because he was Sinatra, it was obvious that we would have a problem enforcing regulations; but when the board came to me, I said, "Go for it!" I told Ed Olsen, "He's no better than anybody else, and you do with him exactly as you would with anyone in that situation. Give no thought to who he is, or who he thinks he is. Do the right thing, and do not be intimidated by him." Sinatra hired an attorney who wrote a couple of threatening letters to me, but the Control Board proceeded against him and he finally gave up his gaming licenses, both at the Cal-Neva and at the Sands. He gave the Sands license up voluntarily when it was made very clear that if he did not, it would be taken from him. Sinatra has spent a lot of years trying to get even.

I later had a brief discussion with President Kennedy about this episode during a short visit he made to Las Vegas. He landed at the airport, and Bible, Cannon, Baring and I all rode with him in an open car to the Convention Center, where he made a speech. He said to me, "What are you guys doing to my friend, Frank Sinatra?"

I said, "Well, Mr. President, I'll try to take care of things here in Nevada, and I wish you luck on the national level." [laughter] That was about the end of that.

7

---

advancing civil rights

There's a vast difference between the way you do things before you are elected and the way you do them after you take office. The nature of politics prevents candidates from making primary points of *every* thing they want to do when they gain office . . . that is, if they hope to get elected, it does. [laughter] You have to use some judgment about what you campaign on. After you're elected, it's a whole different story — you are there for four years, and they'll probably not be able to get rid of you. You begin to devise ways of doing some of the things that you think are really important.

One important thing, as far as I was concerned, was the civil rights issue. When I took office a national movement to improve the situation of minorities in the United States was underway, but I didn't want to wait for federal action — I wanted the state of Nevada to take a position now.[1] The national Democratic party had ignored the issue of segregated facilities, and they ignored the need for affirmative government action to enforce *Brown* v. *Board of Education*.[2] In my view Nevada should go further, and whether anybody else agreed with me really didn't make any difference: I didn't worry about the political fallout. The situation in our state was so shameful that somebody had to step forward and attempt to do something about it, whether it was politically risky or not. Since I would get just one run at this thing, I figured I'd better do all the damage I could do as quickly as I could . . . I might not have another chance.

During my campaign the *San Francisco Chronicle* had accurately summarized my position as fiscally conservative, and liberal on civil rights. My inaugural address articulated those feelings about rights, and called for action:

"In a democracy, there should be no gaps between principles and practices when the civil rights of a man are involved. A community conscience may be apprized by the way it is concerned with those rights and privileges which are guaranteed by law to each individual regardless of his membership in any racial or ethnic group: the right to employment, to education, to housing, to the use of public accommodations, to health and welfare services and facilities, and the right to live in peace and dignity without discrimination, segregation or distinction based on race, religion, color, ancestry, national origin or place of birth."

My address to the first session of the legislature made the same plea, and I moved immediately to get legislation started to create a human relations commission with the authority to investigate civil rights abuses, and the power to take corrective action. To me it was clear that state government had a duty to ensure that all of Nevada's citizens had equal rights, and to do so without delay. Among our legislators, however, there was little sympathy for civil rights, and I had difficulty even finding someone to introduce the bill, which wound up dying in a senate committee. Fortunately, Maude Frazier had the guts to sponsor a second civil rights bill that, while less comprehensive in its objectives, stood a slightly better chance of passing. Assemblywoman Frazier was a remarkable lady, unaffected in the slightest by the political temperature, whatever it was, and totally immune to pressure. She was not answerable to any special interests, which in this case would have meant particularly the gaming industry and contractors and others with a stake in maintaining the racial status quo; she just did what she thought was right. Two days after my state-of-the-state message she introduced AB122, a bill which proposed to outlaw discrimination in public employment and forbid all contractors who did business with the state to discriminate on the grounds of race, national origin, religion, sex, whatever. There was some resistance, particularly in the senate, but the bill eventually passed, and I signed it into law in March.

Although AB122 was a step in the right direction, it was not as strong a piece of civil rights legislation as I had hoped for, because it didn't address the pervasive racism in the private sector. Later that year I received a call from someone in the state department who told me that an ambassador from a black African nation, driving through the West, was attempting to check in to a Nevada hotel and being refused. I called the owner of the establishment and talked to him about the situation. He resisted, but eventually agreed to take care of it. This incident was representative of the overall situation in Nevada. Here, even an official person from another country could not stay in a hotel if he was black, which was so nonsensical that I could hardly believe it! And the hotel owner felt that he could behave that way with impunity until I called him.

Nevada would host the Winter Olympics in 1960, so I issued a public statement at some point to the effect that Nevadans must not, could not in any way, discriminate racially in association with the Olympics. People would be coming to our state from all over the world, and as much as a governor could, I wanted to put a ban on that shoddy practice. This illustrates just how bad the situation was at that time — we had to advocate a special departure from common practice to facilitate an event of worldwide interest. It certainly would have been embarrassing for Nevada to have had segregated hotels and restaurants and so forth which visitors from foreign countries could not patronize if they were black.

And that was the flaw in AB122: it did not address the issues of equal access to public accommodations and equal employment rights in the private sector. This comprised the core of the problem, in my opinion. What do we do about hotels and casinos that blatantly and arrogantly discriminate on the basis of race? The gaming industry thought we should do nothing. They claimed that open accommodations and employment would drive away white patrons, and they had an obsessive fear of being forced to permit blacks to enter casinos as customers . . . or even worse, of having to hire these people as dealers! That mind-set was shared by many legislators, who had been elected with the help and the money of the good-old-boy establishment that was opposed to any of this "socialist" kind of legislation. The argument was foolish. There was no substance to it at all, and even if there had been, it didn't concern me. People in the South were making the same argument, and it was contrary to the ethics and principles of democratic society. If the extension of civil rights resulted in some damage to business, as far as I was concerned that was just an unhappy by-product. Of course, in the end it didn't do any damage, as could have been anticipated from the example provided by the Moulin Rouge

Gov. Sawyer meets with NAACP leaders and other civil rights activists in the capitol. *"Without constant urging from people who were directly involved in the movement, I might not have been as committed as I was to advancing the cause."*

Hotel and Casino in Las Vegas, which had opened in 1955 and for years had been frequented by blacks and whites alike without disturbance. In the early days the Moulin Rouge was the only such place blacks could go. People like Sammy Davis, Lena Horne, and others went there to dine and gamble and so forth when they couldn't be seen except on stage anywhere else in town.

Even though I was highly motivated to extend civil rights to Nevada's black citizens, without constant urging from people who were directly involved in the movement I might not have been as committed as I was to advancing the cause. We got as far as we did in such a relatively short period of time due in large measure to help — not just help, but *forceful* help [laughter] — from members of the Nevada NAACP, whose leadership kept things moving. Their initiative, energy, and resolve enabled us to introduce and pass civil rights legislation before Congress or Jack Kennedy had taken any position on the issue, putting Nevada in the forefront of a social reform issue on which it had long trailed the nation.

Among spokesmen for the NAACP who would come to Carson City to put pressure on state government were Charles Kellar, Eddie Scott, Dr. James McMillan, William H. "Bob" Bailey, and Dr. Charles West. All were on the same team, working for the same objective. Each in his own way was very forceful, but while they were not equals in status and influence, and their efforts sometimes followed divergent paths, these men respected one another. I don't recall ever looking to one specific guy and thinking, "This person will be able to dictate their position." Charlie Kellar was perhaps the most aggressive member of the group, very impatient and demanding. He certainly kept the legislature's attention focused on civil rights, but he could sometimes be abrasive. Eddie Scott, from Reno, was just the opposite, and with his calm composure he was quite an effective advocate and negotiator. So were Drs. West and McMillan, but Bob Bailey may have been the most adept at balancing a passion for justice with an understanding of how to go about getting the system to reform itself. (Bob's son, John R. Bailey, became a lawyer and is now a valued member of the Lionel Sawyer & Collins firm.)

Clyde Mathews and Les Gray, white men, also lobbied very effectively for the cause. Gray was a Republican attorney from Washoe County who had earlier been in the legislature, and he was a strong advocate of civil rights. It was particularly refreshing that a member of the party which historically had been reluctant to make any progress in civil rights was as vocal as Les Gray was about it, and I always admired him for that. Clyde Mathews was a missionary to the Reno-Sparks Indian Colony. He was an accomplished and committed negotiator for civil rights, and was somewhat of a leader of the movement in Nevada in the 1950s and early 1960s. Both of them worked closely with the NAACP.

In the early years of my administration things rarely moved quickly enough to satisfy the civil rights activists, and occasionally they would orchestrate events designed to stimulate action. In 1960 there were a number of sit-ins and demonstrations on the Strip, and in the spring of 1961 the NAACP picketed the capitol to protest continuing discrimination. When the black leadership consulted with me about such actions I rarely attempted to dissuade them; in fact, I encouraged them to go ahead and picket. The unyielding, intransigent style of a few powerful legislators made some form of confrontation necessary.

Clearly, the major obstacle to enacting broad and effective civil rights legislation was the state senate, which was dominated by senators from smaller counties who weren't all that sensitive to urban problems, and who counted few, if any, blacks in their constituencies. With one senator from each county, Clark County had no more representation in the senate than Lincoln or Lyon or the other small counties. Also, the senate historically has been consistently more conservative than the assembly, which tends to elect younger, more progressive people, and although the assembly was willing to come out with a progressive civil rights act, the senate would block it. The senate had some "good old boy" cliques that had been working together for years. Many committees were chaired by men who were anything but progressive, and if a chairman of a major committee (judiciary, for example) was against civil rights, it was going to be difficult to get anything through. While those old boys were tough, however, a number of them relied on the gaming industry for campaign support, and those of us who were pushing for equality for blacks felt that if we could overcome gaming's opposition to civil rights, it would influence some who had been blocking this and other progressive legislation for years. My approach became to make civil rights a factor in gaming licensing, and I was supported and encouraged in this by the leadership of the NAACP.

The governor has leverage and authority in some areas that are crucial to the existence of the gaming industry, and the governor can make some trades. When it became evident that we were not going to get any meaningful civil rights legislation beyond AB122 I convened a meeting of some of the major casino owners in the state, and I told them that whether there was a law or not, so far as the regulation and enforcement of gaming were concerned the policy of the state was that there would not be discrimination in either public accommodations or hiring. I said we would be looking very closely at their operations to determine whether or not the policy of the state was being observed. (In 1963, the attorney general of Nevada, Harvey Dickerson, came with an opinion that I didn't have any authority to do that. But by then I was already doing it, and I continued to do it until we had a law that took care of the situation.) As governor, I was in a strong position on this issue: I appointed all the regulators and controllers of the gaming industry — the people who granted gaming licenses and had the power to revoke them or limit them or place conditions on them. Even those operators who had been licensed before I took office were subject to control and regulation, and that made them very careful about taking positions that might displease the regulators. And I told the industry that we were going to appoint some black gaming agents. [laughter]

There are some broad, generic terms in the gaming regulations, such as "unsuitable methods of operation"[3] that can be used in calling a licensee up for a hearing . . . and any number of business practices or procedures (and we are talking here specifically about denial of employment rights and access to public accommodations) could be determined to be not in the best interests of the state. A licensee was going to pay close attention when the governor said, "Now, this is the policy of this state. I am appointing people to the Gaming Control Board and the Gaming Commission who understand the policy and are going to be expecting licensees to put it into effect. If you don't, we may want to have a hearing on your license." So that's where I started — I felt that once these people were won over, the rest of it would naturally develop, which it did.

After 1960 both political parties were taking strong civil rights positions nationally. The impetus for this came from the national leadership, which with social issues usually doesn't work, but in this case it did. And politicians were reluctant to publicly buck a popular president of the United States, because it might affect their next election. In fact I believe, perhaps cynically, that *most* of the civil rights votes by office holders came not from principle, but with an eye on their next election. In Nevada, I had been elected with a very substantial majority, and even those people who wanted to publicly differ with me on civil rights were not nearly as open as they might have been under other circumstances . . . they didn't want me campaigning against them the next time they ran. Self-preservation was the bottom line. [laughter]

In 1961 we got a law that set up the Nevada Civil Rights Commission.[4] The commission had little, if any, funding or statutory authority, and I think it also lacked subpoena power. Nevertheless it set some goals and enunciated a position that the legislature had previously refused to take. Establishing the commission was the first legislative act that demonstrated an interest in the civil rights of the general population, rather than just in the relations between state government and the public; but in truth the Nevada legislative establishment was still hostile toward civil rights — they were not crazy about my position on any legislation in this area.

In the next legislative session there was a threat to abolish the commission, which was countered by Assemblywoman Flora Dungan's move to strengthen it. The senate, which had always been a bulwark of anti-civil rights feeling, had finally, and reluctantly, helped create this commission in 1961, but they hadn't given it any money or any teeth; and then in 1963 they used the excuse that since it wasn't doing anything . . . . It was an interesting turn of events: "We shaped something so that it wouldn't work, and now because it isn't working we are going to abolish it!" Fortunately that didn't happen. But the effort to strengthen the commission also failed, due to the attitude of leaders like state senator Jim Slattery, who claimed that blacks living in Nevada had never been so well off, and that they even drove better cars than he did![5] [laughter] As the paid senator of the gaming industry in Reno, Slattery made no bones about being against civil rights legislation — he was there to represent his patrons, and he did it very well, expressing views that were typical of that interest.

Some time ago, in the *Nevada Public Affairs Review*, I was criticized for my handling of the civil rights commission.[6] The suggestion that I dragged my feet on an issue in which I take great pride of accomplishment was personally offensive to me. While technically some of the things that were written were correct, the authors had no idea what was going on behind the scenes, and had they checked, I'm sure they would have understood that there were certain things that I couldn't do. For example, when the legislature created the commission in the first place but gave it no money, that hamstrung it. And making more aggressive use of the Gaming Commission to advance racial equality would have been impossible. The primary duty of the Gaming Commission was not to enforce civil rights in the state of Nevada — that was a side agenda which I personally was following. And there were many other things that I could not do because we did not have the necessary legislation on the books.

The NAACP in Nevada became so frustrated by the ineffectiveness of the civil rights commission that it came out in support of jail terms for discriminatory practices, but we were still struggling just to get a decent commission with some power and authority, and to jump all the way into criminal penalties was a leap forward that wasn't practical. My feeling was that there could be an opportunity to make the commission more effective by establishing some civil penalties for discrimination, but there was no chance of getting the system to accept criminal penalties.

Pickets protest the state senate's reluctance to pass effective civil rights legislation, 1963. *"As the paid senator of the gaming industry in Reno, Slattery made
no bones about being against civil rights legislation."*

A demonstration to protest employment discrimination on the Strip was planned to coincide with the Liston-Patterson heavyweight championship fight in July 1963. I was in New York City on state business at the time, but when the situation got a little inflamed Bob Bailey called and asked me to cut my visit short and return to Las Vegas immediately. He and some others met me at the Las Vegas airport and drove me to a meeting between civil rights activists and representatives of Strip hotel-casinos. I told the businessmen that it was high time to end their discriminatory practices, and in a mediating effort I also made some recommendations to the Westside[7] leadership, not to abate what they wanted to do, but to diminish the sensational aspects of it if we could.

The threat of a demonstration that would disrupt the business brought by a title fight gave me a little more leverage with the hotels and casinos than I had had in past efforts to deal with the problem, and I felt that we were in a strong bargaining position at that point: "If this demonstration does not occur, what will you do to help alleviate the situation?" And with the folks who wanted to demonstrate, I had to give some assurances that there would be good-faith dealings with the other side to open up some of the areas that we were concerned about. A demonstration in Las Vegas would hurt Nevada's reputation nationally, and if we could accomplish something solid without one, even if it was a compromise, that was the way I wanted to approach it. And I did. Along with Oran Gragson and Hank Greenspun and others, I talked to both sides, and we brokered a compromise between them, and the demonstration did not occur.

As part of this settlement, casino owners finally agreed to start hiring some blacks in non-menial positions, including management, but years later we got into an argument over whether this policy extended to top management or just "management" — we hadn't been too precise in our terms. Casinos had started to hire people to fill accounting and other positions in administrative offices of hotel-casinos, which had never been done before, but these positions were generally not as visible to the public as some others. After the 1964 federal civil rights act passed, I never again heard of any failure to accept people of all races and colors in public accommodations in Nevada;[8] however, there are *still* perceived to be some problems with respect to employment of blacks in management positions, although there are relatively few complaints anymore to the commission. As a matter of fact, black employment in managerial positions in Nevada may now be proportionate to the number of blacks in the state's population. Things have come along fairly well, but of course they could be better; they could be better everywhere in the country, not just in Nevada.

8

water, land and the government

Disputes between Nevada and California over state boundaries go back to the days of the Comstock Lode. During my administration the debate centered on assigning responsibility for protecting Lake Tahoe and the land around it. Casino construction and operation on the Nevada side were affecting the quality of the lake, but there was also a good deal of damage being done by the lumber industry and by general construction, both in Nevada *and* in California. When land was disturbed in order to build a new casino, or a new house, or whatever, debris would wash down into the lake, and over a period of time that led to deterioration in the clarity and color of the water, diminishing its usefulness for swimming, boating, and other types of recreation. There was also a significant pollution problem caused by leaking septic tanks and illegal campers, and other damage was being done by people who were just generally destructive of the environment.

California Governor Pat Brown and I recognized that we had a problem, so we got together to explore various ways that our two states could cooperate to save Lake Tahoe from unrestrained development. We discussed issues of property rights, water development rights, environmental problems, and so forth; but although we understood the urgency of doing something about preserving the lake, and we acknowledged that Nevada and California shared responsibility, each of us was also trying to protect his own turf. I became a little annoyed when Pat complained that the lake was being ruined by sewage from Nevada. My response was he must believe that Californians don't defecate! [laughter] Lake Tahoe lies 70 percent within California and 30 percent within Nevada, and proportionately, growth on the California side had been much greater. With federal approval, a California/Nevada Bi-State Commission was eventually set up. It had teeth, and it successfully restricted growth on both sides of the border to the point where the hotels and casinos now at Lake Tahoe are the last ones we will see.

In an unrelated attempt to address the problem of saving the lake, Senator Alan Bible sponsored legislation to create a national park on the Nevada side, and I backed him in his efforts. In spite of my bias against the federal bureaucracy, the situation was so urgent that I would have welcomed federal protection of that pristine area . . . anything to halt the destruction. In 1961 Interior Secretary Stewart Udall visited the lake, and Alan Bible, Howard Cannon, and I went along with him. Udall supported Bible's proposal, but the idea of a national park on the lake never seemed to take hold.

Although it was almost too late on the California shore, I was determined to preserve as much undeveloped land as we could on the Nevada side of the lake, even without federal

Edmund "Pat" Brown, governor of California, meets with newly-inaugurated Gov.
Grant Sawyer of Nevada, 1959.

help. If we could establish a state park on our east shore beaches, not only would it check environmental destruction, it would also preserve for public use the land that was rapidly being gobbled up by private interests. George Whittell[1] controlled most of the Nevada shore, so I pursued him, hoping he would give us (or sell to us at reduced prices) some of that beach property that we wanted to set aside.

Whittell was extremely wealthy, and he owned a big castle out by the lake with lions and elephants and a bunch of exotic things there. He was almost a mythical figure, but one who didn't answer his telephone — nobody ever knew where he was. When I called, he wouldn't talk to me, so I sent out spies to try to find him. They learned where he lived in California, and I flew there on a secret mission and went out to his house and met his wife . . . but I didn't get any further than the kitchen, and she refused to let me speak to him, although I knew very well that he was in the house. We finally got funding from the Fleischmann Foundation, and with some legislative appropriations, land was purchased for the first portion of what is now the Nevada state park at Lake Tahoe. I think when Governor Laxalt came in, he added another piece either by direct appropriation of the legislature or through a grant of some kind. It's a pretty fair state park now.

I was proud of my administration's efforts to protect Lake Tahoe, but I can't claim sole possession of that issue — the men who immediately preceded and succeeded me as governor were aware of the problem, and took measures as well; I just helped move things along. A lot of people opposed our actions, but we managed to start the saving of Lake Tahoe back in those years, and it was worth earning the resentment of our opponents. That is one of the most gorgeous areas in the world.

Oddly enough, in the last year or two people have suddenly begun to say, "Oh, my gosh. We've got a water problem!" Thirty years ago I was saying that. Recently, in preparing for the oral history interviews from which this book is derived, I reviewed some of my monthly reports to voters that were filmed and distributed to television stations while I was governor. One of those programs was on water, and even then I was warning that we had to have a massive infusion of it if Nevada was to continue to develop . . . and that we had to conserve and perfect the use of the water to which we already had access.

In 1961, southern Nevada was already in trouble because of population growth. Water and power sources were inadequate, and it was clear that the day would come — it actually came sooner than most people expected — when this was going to be a very serious problem. We were aware that some long-range planning had to be done. It wasn't then politically possible to do anything at the local or state levels, but we had a study done, and later we got the Southern Nevada Water Project[2] with federal funding, primarily because of Senator Bible's influence. The project was a boost, providing enough water for development into the 1990s, but a lot more should have been done in those years. I won't say we're too late now, but it's pretty far along in the game to be talking to the community about importing water from Nevada's northern counties. You just can't convince people to do something about water until they turn on the faucets and nothing comes out.

Water was always on my mind as the one potentially insurmountable obstacle to the continued development and growth of this state, and I wasn't concerned about the environmental impact of tapping in to sources of it. I wasn't worried about the welfare of snails or pupfish or anything else; I was concerned about doing something which would permit this state to continue to grow, even twenty or thirty years later, and as governor I supported most federal reclamation projects in the West. Some controversy surrounded the possibility of federal assistance in solving Nevada's water problems, however. Over 80 percent of this state was already in federal hands — at least the land rights were — and there was concern that with a federal reclamation project would come federal laws. Opinion has been shifting back and forth for decades as to who controls what water at various times. I preferred the old legal maxim that states control all the water within their borders, but there are certain instances in which that does not apply, and whether I wanted it to or not didn't make any difference. Even though the Colorado River passes through a sliver of Nevada, courts had long ago decided that the state could not control its flow at that point because other states were involved as well. The only possible way we were going to get our share of the Colorado was by federal court action.

When the Colorado River decision finally came down in 1963, Nevada got pretty short shrift, receiving 300,000 acre feet of water per annum as its share. Had anyone then dreamed what was going to happen to southern Nevada, I suppose they would have tried to get more; but I am not critical of anybody who was involved in that litigation, which went on for over a decade. We had asked originally for 500,000 acre feet; however, even with the inflated figures that Hugh Shamberger put into Nevada's brief, he was dead wrong in terms of the number of people that would be here by the year 2000. No one could have anticipated what was going to happen, but if we'd received even the amount we requested, we could probably go on for another twenty or thirty years with the kind of growth we are having now. As it is, we can't go that far unless drastic steps are taken to get the water from other areas.[3]

In northern Nevada the problem is that the Truckee, Carson, and Walker Rivers originate in California and flow into Nevada, where they terminate. In 1960 Nevada and California got permission from the federal government to try to decide who gets what from the flow of each river, but the negotiations went on for years and years — the issue wasn't even decided while I was in office. I met with Governor Brown a number of times on that, and while we were each representing our constituents the best we could, we knew the dispute had to be settled . . . some way or another the matter had to be resolved.

There were other potential sources of water for Nevada. I went to Oregon and met with its governor and tried to enter into an interstate compact to bring some Columbia River water down into Nevada — Idaho was involved in that as well — but I didn't get to first base. Water is so precious that nobody was going to give any up . . . even though the Columbia River dumps millions of acre feet into the Pacific every year while Nevada and California are starving for water! I didn't get anywhere with that idea; and anyway, an interstate compact to facilitate it would have required the approval of congress. I would support any scheme that would give us more water, and we even tried to get some from Alaska through the Cascade Project. But not only would that have required congressional approval, it would also have depended upon a massive infusion of federal funds to build a system to transport that water.

The wars that Nevada has had with the federal government over use of public lands arise from a peculiar condition. When Nevada and eight other western states were admitted to the Union, the Union retained ownership and control of the public lands in those states based on the theory that their populations were so small that they would not be able to use or manage these lands. Now, you don't find any of this in the rest of the country — it was just out here in the West. The people of New Jersey own their public lands; they do in Pennsylvania; they do in Ohio . . . but not in Nevada, or Utah, or Idaho, or Alaska! I almost have an obsession about this inequitable treatment.

Notwithstanding my position on federal ownership of our land, I favored the creation of additional national parks in the West, and in particular the Great Basin National Park in Nevada. Many constituents did not share my enthusiasm. Nevada's mining interests and livestock industry (supported by my lieutenant governor, Paul Laxalt) were opposed to the Great Basin park because it would end access to land that they had been using for a number of years. This was short-sighted and selfish.

Senator Alan Bible, who was in a very powerful position on the Interior Committee, sponsored the bill to create a park, but Walter Baring countered with a proposal for a much smaller one. Baring, in my opinion, was representing the mining and ranching interests. If we were to have a park, it should be a decent-sized one, and I supported Bible's efforts. Although it is smaller than I had hoped, I was happy when the park was finally established because it protects a spectacular area and at the same time is good for the economic health of the state.[4]

While I found myself on the side of the livestock people on the issue of ownership of public lands, I could *not* support a Nevada resolution denouncing Secretary Udall for his policy of increasing grazing fees. Although I disagreed with Udall, he was a close friend, and I admired and respected him. He was doing his job as he saw it, and to personally attack him at that point was ill advised, especially since we were seeking concessions for our bi-state Lake Tahoe compact and other matters important to Nevada. I wanted to maintain a good working relationship with Udall, and I didn't think making personal attacks on him was the way to do that . . . or the way to solve any issue.

After becoming governor I got exercised over the fact that one hundred and ten thousand square miles of Nevada really wasn't under my control at all, and I made my concern known at the federal level. Quickly the message came back that this was not our land, it was theirs. Well, what are they going to do with it? Whatever they do has to have our consent, and if they develop any land, they have to buy it from us. It seemed absurd to me that although Nevada had grown and was able to control its own destiny and to develop its own infra-structures, its centers of population were still surrounded by millions of acres of empty land that the state did not own; so I presented the Western Conference of Governors with a resolution to Congress to allow the states to purchase BLM land. Later, I made the same appeal to the National Governors' Conference. Governors outside the West have no comprehension; they don't know what we are yelling about. You tell them, "Look, 87 percent of my state is still owned by the federal government," and they are shocked.

In 1960 The Multiple Use-Sustained Yield Act was passed by Congress, and it made sense to me.[5] I did not object to the idea that certain areas should be set aside for recreational purposes. But to continue to control all the public land and say, "If you want any of this, you're going to have to deal with us; even though your cities are bursting at the seams and you have no place to grow, nobody can buy or develop that land . . . . " Let us go! You are treating us like serfs out here. You gave us a bit of land to start with, but you still have over 80 percent of the total, and we've outgrown the little that we got. We're civilized and we need to develop. The federally-controlled public lands in Nevada should be put on the public market!

9

---

a second term:
reform is validated

My first term as governor had been an exciting four years, and it was rewarding in many respects. But as anyone would in that job, I would have liked to accomplish a lot more than I did. Being relatively naive, I was frustrated — we had made substantial progress with gaming regulation, but not without taking a lot of heat; advances in civil rights came painfully slowly; and although we got reorganization of state government, that was just a structural change, about which it was hard to get passionate. People don't live for structural change! I hoped to build on our accomplishments with a second term.

The campaign of 1962 was unusual: Lieutenant Governor Rex Bell announced his candidacy for governor, but he died before the primaries. Rex's death saddened all of us, and it was quite a blow to the Republican party, which still managed to mount a credible challenge — in the Republican primary Oran Gragson ran a spirited campaign against Hank Greenspun, winning handily and becoming my opponent in the general election. I knew Oran reasonably well (he was mayor of Las Vegas), and I liked him. He was a true gentleman who had none of the sleaze about him that you run into with some candidates. It's unusual to finish a campaign without developing some rancor toward your opponent, but I never did toward Oran. We got along very well afterwards and right up to the present. That would have been difficult had Rex Bell been the candidate.

Oran was hard for me to campaign against because he was kind of like Maude Frazier: he was a distinguished mayor who had done a fine job, and he was highly respected. It was never my style to be personally critical of an opponent, anyway, and I didn't even necessarily differ with Oran's views. The only thing I had a little difficulty with was public appearances when we would share a platform. It was Oran's misfortune to have a speech defect . . . while I was often accused of being too glib. He would speak, and people would be very sympathetic — everybody straining to help him — and then I would get up and come off as a city slicker. I sometimes thought I had better make a few mistakes so there wouldn't be such a wide contrast. [laughter]

During the campaign a nasty leaflet was distributed that was uncomplimentary towards Mayor Gragson, highlighting his speech problem. This type of thing is endemic to political campaigns, and there were a lot of nasty items floating around about me, as well. One little booklet was spread all over: it was entitled, "What Has Grant Sawyer Done for the State of Nevada?" and you open the thing and it's all blank pages. [laughter] Usually the candidates themselves don't have much to do with these things; it's generally the work of some over-zealous supporter, and if I had suspected anyone in our camp of being responsible for the leaflet ridiculing Oran's speech, I would have had a talk with him. What's fair is fair. There has to be some ethical and moral basis to the way we treat each other, even in a campaign.

I won reelection by a margin of 32,000 votes, which shocked me. Although Oran had gone into this exercise at a great disadvantage (he couldn't reasonably have been expecting to win), with all the fire that I'd been under for four years I was surprised that I could win by that margin. But I wasn't deluded: the vote was less attributable to my charm and popularity than to circumstances such as Rex Bell's death and other things. Even so, it gave me a lot of comfort. It resolved whatever lingering doubts I may have had about the controversial positions I had taken on civil rights and gaming control over the preceding four years.

In 1962 I campaigned for all the Democrats. We formed a caravan and went around the state supporting all who were running for state offices, including Berkeley Bunker, who was running for lieutenant governor against Paul Laxalt, a very attractive candidate. Laxalt certainly had strong support from the Republican party, which was beginning to close the registered-voters gap with the Democrats, although the Democrats still had a substantial margin. Berkeley was virtually unknown in the north, while Paul was very strong in the north because he came from there; when Paul won I was not particularly surprised.

I had had a reasonably satisfactory experience with Rex Bell, and I was unconcerned about my ability to govern with Paul Laxalt as my lieutenant governor. Clearly, however, I did not have the same relationship with Mr. Laxalt that I had enjoyed with Mr. Bell, and following the first few months that he was in office, I didn't have any discussions with him on issues. It would have been fruitless. After several early attempts to talk with him — not necessarily to convince him of my point of view, but usually to work on problems affecting the state — I learned that there was no such thing as a private meeting with Mr. Laxalt: any discussion we had was almost invariably relayed to the press, or in some other fashion made public. Therefore for the rest of my second term I didn't discuss things with Laxalt, whereas with Rex Bell, I could.

Stories soon began to appear speculating that Laxalt's victory over Bunker precluded my running for the Senate against Howard Cannon in 1964, because that would elevate a Republican to the governor's chair — in short, Laxalt's victory had boxed me in. But I never had any intention of running against Cannon. My theory then and now is that if you have people from a small state like Nevada who are doing a good job in the United States Senate, you better leave them there so they'll gain some seniority, because that's the way the game is played. If you are constantly changing senators, you just dilute the power of your state. Nevada has as many people in the Senate as bigger states like New York, California, New Jersey, Pennsylvania — two from each state — and if they're good people doing a good job, ultimately you are going to gain the positions of power: the committee chairmanships. That's the way our government runs, and the reason that the South has always fared so well is because historically they have elected people to the Senate and left them there. A few years ago, most of the major chairmanships in the Senate were held by southerners for that reason.

For me to run against Howard Cannon or any other established, competent office holder would have been the sleaziest, most self-serving kind of politics, and I never considered running for the Senate despite all the stories to the contrary. But Paul Laxalt did, and that turned out to be one of the closest elections in Nevada history.[1] I supported Cannon one *thousand* percent, because by that time I had gotten to know Laxalt pretty well! And Cannon had been doing a very good job in the Senate regardless of what the press said.

Politically more significant than the Cannon-Laxalt contest were the reapportionment cases of the early 1960s. Specifically, two rulings of the United States Supreme Court, *Baker* v. *Carr* (1962) and *Reynolds* v. *Sims* (1964), dictated one man, one vote. State legislatures had to be apportioned solely on the basis of population, which meant that states like Nevada, which followed the "Little Federal Plan" (all counties entitled to the same number of senators) would have to reapportion. You could like this or not, but it was the law of the land.

Nevada experienced quite a political upheaval, and the outcry in all the counties but Clark and Washoe was shrill, to say the least, because most Nevadans were comfortable with one senator from each county, each ostensibly having equal say and equal authority. Actually, the small counties up to that time had totally controlled the state senate with seniority: as in the United States Senate, seniority was nearly everything, and although one-man-one-vote was a boon to Clark and Washoe, it stripped some counties of their power in the legislature and left the smallest ones with virtually no representation. (That's still the case today.) A lot of very bitter people fought it to the last ditch — small counties were losing their champions, and powerful, vested interests (particularly mining and cattle), who essentially had had their own state senators representing them for many years, were fresh out of luck. On the other hand, those interested in social legislation — civil rights, et cetera — now saw a possibility for legislative determinations in that area. There was a lot of pulling and hauling both ways.

From a purely political standpoint, Democrats in Nevada had more to gain from one-man-one-vote than Republicans. In those days registration in Clark County was about three-to-one Democrats over Republicans, so just on that basis Democrats had more to gain . . . and Washoe County was slightly Democrat over Republican. Many small counties were Republican, and some of those districts were in danger of being gobbled up, and that's the way it worked out. My attitude was simply, "What difference does it make? This is now the law of the land, and there is nothing we can do about it." But Flora Dungan, then an assemblywoman, filed suit in federal court to *force* Nevada to implement the Supreme Court ruling.[2] She won, and the federal court ordered Nevada to reapportion.

I did not see reapportionment as a federal attack on states' rights, as Paul Laxalt argued that it was. There was a clear difference between what we called states' rights in those days and the right of Americans to be represented in the legislative affairs of their states, and we had a situation in Nevada where many of our people were not represented. Even in 1964, the black citizens of Nevada still had not received their full complement of American citizenship. There was no contradiction between my states' rights position — which I still hold, by the way — and demanding that all citizens have equal access to their government and their society, and I never understood Laxalt on that: his was purely a political position, in my opinion. He was representing, as he always had, a lot of vested interests, and he did not agree with me on social issues. Paul Laxalt was just fanning the breeze of public resentment.

Laxalt also claimed that Nevada was in danger of losing its two United States senators. That was totally ridiculous! What the Supreme Court had done had no application to the United States Senate at all — the makeup of the Senate was controlled by clear constitutional provisions, and there could be no judicial decision in that respect. But it's very difficult to convey those nuances to the public, so a lot of times I just had to sit silent, comfortable in the knowledge that Laxalt didn't know what the hell he was talking about. To me, it was quite simple: Regarding one-man-one-vote there was nothing to fight about. The Court had declared it, and that was it . . . unless the people wanted to go through the process of amending the Constitution.

Once it was clear that we had to do it, I preferred that the Nevada legislature reapportion itself rather than have the district court in Las Vegas put together a plan. Our legislators were more representative of our people than appointed judges, and reluctant though they were, they had little choice — they were going to have to bite the bullet. I appointed a commission of fifteen, chaired by Attorney General Harvey Dickerson, to study the problem of implementation and make recommendations as to how to proceed. Then I called a special session of the legislature to deal with reapportionment. All kinds of plans came out during the special session, because many legislators tried to save their own positions. You can't blame them for that. They finally created an assembly of forty members and a senate of twenty, and that proportion remains in effect today — not the number, but the proportion. Clark County got eight of the twenty senators, and Washoe and Storey counties got six. Eureka, Humboldt, Lander and Pershing each received one senator; Esmeralda, Mineral and Nye combined got one senator; there are some others where two counties got one senator. That was a tremendous change. Clark County received almost half the seats, whereas before it had been on the same level of power with Lincoln, White Pine, Lander, Humboldt and Pershing.

This was a major shift in power, and there were dire prophesies of doom: the whole state would be a slave to the gaming industry in Clark County, and so on. But the gaming interests didn't acquire any more power through reapportionment than they had before, and maybe in a way they lost representation. When Nevada had a limited number of senators, one from each county, most of them were very responsive to the gaming industry. Now, the need to spread the action around among more people means that gaming is less likely to get subservience from a number of them, even though they support their candidacies financially. And I don't think that Clark County since 1964 has run as roughshod over mining and livestock interests as many feared it would — there hasn't been any stomach for it on the part of Clark legislators. Small counties may not agree with my assessment, but I think that on the whole, representatives from Clark County have leaned over backwards to be fair. Some thirty years later, the bitterness northern Nevada feels toward southern Nevada is still as great as in 1964, but I don't think it's entirely based on one-man, one-vote — a lot of other ingredients go into it.

One bit of fallout from the Supreme Court's decisions led to the end of Nevada's influence in the Democratic party: the Democratic National Committee decided that its delegates, too, should be apportioned on a one-man, one-vote basis. The committee had been organized in the fashion of the United States Senate, with each state's Democrats electing one man and one woman to represent them on it; and under that system if you had the ability, you could become a real player, regardless of what state you were from. But when they decided to reapportion, Nevada was suddenly pushed almost to the bottom of the heap on the basis of its small population. While states like New York wound up with thirty delegates, as did California, New Jersey, and Pennsylvania, Nevada suddenly became a non-player on the national party level, and it has remained so to this day.

In 1964 I was elected chairman of the National Governors' Conference, the only Nevada governor ever elected to that position.[3] Although the vote was unanimous, my victory was not necessarily because I was such an outstanding governor — there was a lot of politics in this, as always. Governors of some large states were vying for the position, and it became sort of a stand-off. Finally they said, "Hell, let's go with Sawyer; he can't hurt anybody, and he isn't competitive with New York or Pennsylvania or California." It was also probably noted that I wasn't up for reelection for another two years, and could actually give some time to the organization.

The way things worked in those days was that when the president of the United States was in your party, he ran virtually every matter of this kind. Lyndon Johnson controlled the Democratic National Committee, he appointed his people to run the party, and anything like my election to the chairmanship of the National Governors' Conference would have had to receive his tacit blessing. In fact, in most political issues that came before the national governors, White House representatives at the conferences would pass the party line. They'd say, "This is what the president wants," and sometimes you would just go with that as a matter of pure politics. But although my relationship with President Johnson at that point was pretty good, and he must have accepted my election — there was no animosity left from 1960, when I had supported Jack Kennedy against him — I doubt that he was actively either for or against my becoming chairman. Johnson was a true politician, and when something was over, it was over: "Today's enemies are tomorrow's allies."

The next National Governors' Conference meeting was held in San Juan, Puerto Rico. All the governors stayed in one hotel, outside of which three or four hundred people, *independistas,* assembled to picket and complain about United States policy toward Puerto Rico. The conference staff got everybody together and said, "We're going to cancel our tour agenda right now. We don't want any big incidents, and we suggest you just lay low until this thing is over." But I was curious, so I went out to see what was going on and found myself in the middle of the rally, the only governor out there . . . which I guess was sort of foolish. The *independistas* spotted me and insisted that I say a few words. I told them that we each have the right to take any position we want, and if they felt that independence was the proper course for Puerto Rico, they certainly had the right to say so. I encouraged them to do what they thought was best for their country, because that's the way democracy works. They thought that was terrific! I hadn't really said anything, but the fact that someone came out and addressed them pleased them, and the rally broke up not too long after that.

Crime control was a major political issue in the mid 1960s, with Nevada reported by the FBI to have the highest per capita crime rate in the nation. I took exception. The FBI had taken the population of Nevada and said x number of crimes were committed in the state in a given year; therefore, Nevada was number one percentage-wise. But this didn't take into account crimes by transients. On any given day there could be as many crimes committed in Nevada by people from out of state as by criminals who lived here permanently. We were the biggest tourist state in the country, comparing permanent population with the number of tourists who visit annually, and it seemed obvious to me that the crime statistics, to be valid, should include some factor to show that many crimes were committed by tourists and other transients. Apparently the FBI didn't see it that way.

To address Nevada's problem with transient crime, I wanted to establish a state Bureau of Criminal Identification and Investigation. We did not have very effective interstate communication about the identities and criminal records of prisoners and suspects; nor did we have effective communication with federal law enforcement authorities — indeed, Nevada was sort of operating in a vacuum, with no way of knowing whether someone apprehended here had already been arrested in ten other states or for a federal crime. I wanted to bring us up to speed on quick and effective communication, and establish an operation similar to those in other states, with fingerprint analysis, et cetera. But it never happened. Reluctant to fund it, the assembly wouldn't vote a bill to create such an agency.

I also supported an Early Prisoner Release Bill in 1965, calling for the release of a certain class of prisoners before they had served their minimum amount of time. I could see what was happening: you can't just put people in prison and leave them there for a specified period, regardless of their potential for rehabilitation; if you do that, you just continue to build prisons, and even then Nevada was incarcerating more people per capita than any other state in the Union. Many in our prisons were kids, or had committed a crime for the first time, but by the time they got out after years of incarceration they were lost to society. There has to be a better way, unless we just want to spend the taxpayers' dollars the rest of our lives building new prisons and warehousing these people. I felt that the system should use some judgment as to when to get those people back into productive life.

Although I think time has shown that I was right, the bill was quickly dubbed the "early-parole bill" by my opponents, and district attorneys were by and large greatly opposed to it. They felt that I was interfering with their prerogatives — some of them wanted to get criminals into prison and leave them in there forever. Also at that point people were looking for political soft spots in me, because we were getting ready for the next big political season, the campaign of 1966. People like Bill Raggio in Reno and Ted Marshall, who was district attorney in Las Vegas, saw a political opportunity and made the most of it. (Marshall ultimately ran against me.) They talked about letting rapists out on the street to rape your sister or your mother — all of these horror stories.

To be perceived as soft on crime is deadly to a politician, and the whole thing was very damaging to me. There was a lot of conversation about the bill, a lot of press, and a lot of distortion, and it was just too complicated an issue to discuss with the public and say, "Now, look. Don't you agree with me?" It was one of those Willie Horton things, making me easily labelled "soft on crime," a charge that was difficult to counter.[4] People were saying that I had forgotten my days as a district attorney, but even as a DA I had had doubts about the system.

Besides all the issues and legislative problems, the governor must deal with interest groups and their lobbyists. Many of the positions that various pressure groups take are conflicting, and the worst thing you can do is try to satisfy everybody, because it can't be done. You just come off as a weak wimp who is putting his finger in the wind on every issue. You get to the point, and I guess I did, where you listen to everybody and make up your own mind and hope for the best. I frequently took what were considered anti-labor and anti-gaming positions, and I was not always receptive to cattlemen or mining, either, because all these groups tend to take extreme positions. Unless you have some independence and use your own judgment, you can't survive, because every time you make a decision somebody's mad at you. Your enemies never forget, and your friends think that whatever you did for them, you owed it to them . . . that's just the way it goes. [laughter]

In those days organized labor, and particularly the culinary union, had a lot more leverage than it does today. Principals in that union held important Democratic party positions, particularly in Las Vegas, and they controlled their members and were able to turn out the vote pretty well. They could offer a candidate a lot of assistance in voter registration, and could provide some free stuff that otherwise you would have to pay for in a campaign. When labor came along and took a unified position on something, they had a lot of clout. In northern Nevada, the Cattlemen's Association and the mining industry were important; and statewide, the gaming industry carried a lot of clout, because that's where most of the money came from for major political candidates. However, unlike today, teachers were relatively unimportant as an interest group, which makes me prouder of what we accomplished in support of education — in those days we were second only to California in the West on the various indices that were used to measure the quality of education: money, teacher-student ratios, and high test scores.

As with some other issues, part of the reason for supporting education so strongly was our concern about the image of the state. To the credit of Governor Russell, Nevada's image in the area of education was reasonably high when I was elected, and I intended to keep it that way, but I soon began experiencing difficulties with the legislature, which was reluctant to go along with the program. Twice in eight years, unsatisfied with what they did in the regular sessions, I had to call them back for special sessions and urge them to appropriate more money for education. By 1966, when I was running for a third term, 69 percent of the total budget for the state of Nevada was being spent on education. We had raised teachers' and professors' salaries, and we had appropriated funds for construction of some nineteen buildings on the campuses of the University of Nevada and Nevada Southern. In our efforts on behalf of education, Senator Mahlon Brown from Las Vegas was a legislative leader. He was particularly adept at getting appropriations for Nevada Southern increased, and he led the fight to keep the campus that became UNLV on the path of progressive, dramatic growth.

M y staff did some creative things with television, and political opponents were quick to charge that I was using this for political purposes. Indeed, I was. [laughter] Actually, the programs which we broadcast served two purposes — to inform the public and to put forward my political position — and I don't think we ever used any state funds for television presentations. All TV was live in those days, so when you did a program you had to be "on" — it could be disastrous if you weren't, because the moment you said something, it was on the air! Since my programs were on the volatile issues of the day, sometimes it would have been easier to just sit silent and say nothing and avoid controversy. But I enjoyed doing television.

By and large the media were fair to me. Over the years, there were just a few occasions when I got mad enough about something reported in a newspaper to pick up the phone and talk to an editor, and those were early on in my career. Later I learned it's a total waste of time, and you just have to suffer in silence. [laughter]

Just before I was to address the legislature after my second election I contracted hepatitis, and we were concerned about how to handle it. You can't conceal it, because you turn yellow, so we figured it had to be announced to the press. Lovelock had a little paper, the *Review-Miner*, which was very black Republican, and anti-Sawyer all the way through. [laughter] The *Review-Miner* carried the story on its front page, and everybody was wondering what hepatitis is — some people thought it was like cirrhosis of the liver or venereal disease or something. Someone wrote, "This is what it is: it's a disease that loud-mouthed politicians pick up from dirty toilet stools." [laughter]

On another occasion I had planned to go to a fund-raising ball for the heart association, but while having dinner with some friends before the affair I became violently ill. (In fact, I vomited all over the restaurant.) They hauled me out of there and took me back to my motel and called a doctor, so I never did appear at the ball. The next morning on the front page of the *Las Vegas Review-Journal* there was a black-lined story saying that I had been at the ball; that I had appeared to have had a lot to drink; that I insulted the stars who were in the receiving line at the ball; and that the whole thing was a disaster. [laughter]

In those early days of my administration I was still pretty naive, so I called the editor of the paper, John Cahlan, and said, "John, I just read this story. Where did you get your information?"

He said, "I got it from an unimpeachable source."

I asked, "Was this unimpeachable source there? Did he actually see all of these things that you are recounting?"

John said, "Unimpeachable!"

So I just said, "Well, John, I was never there." I told him that I had been ill; I had a doctor's affidavit at that point.

He said, "Well, we have to sell papers."

Similar things happened to me later, but after that experience I said, "Hell, there's no point whatsoever in calling the
editor of a newspaper if you don't like the way a story is
written. You just take your chances, pot luck, and hope it
comes out right."

10

nevada's first three-term governor ?

Coming into the election of 1966 the party organization was generally behind me. Polls indicated that I was the only Democrat who could win, so appeals were made to my loyalty to the party, and I finally decided to run for a third term. But it turned out that support from within the party was not all that it could have been. Ted Marshall, the district attorney in Las Vegas, decided to oppose me in the primary. So did Charlie Springer.

In 1962, when Attorney General Roger Foley was tapped for the federal district court in Las Vegas, I had chosen Charlie Springer to replace him. (He was a good lawyer, but I chose him primarily because he did not intend to be a candidate for the office in the fall elections that year . . . I didn't want to give a potential contender the unfair advantage of running as an incumbent.) Charlie was an appealing young progressive

Democrat, and I sort of took him under my wing, until suddenly in 1966 he announced his candidacy for governor and made some vicious charges against me. I was bewildered. He had never given any indication that he disapproved of anything I was doing, and the savagery of his attack was startling . . . but it didn't startle me as much as the fact that he was running for governor. [laughter] He was very rough on me. Of course, that's politics — if he was going to run, you wouldn't expect him to run just for the exercise.

Springer charged that gaming interests had given me $100,000 for my campaign in 1962, his point being not that they bought influence by so doing, but that I had deceived the electorate by not coming forward about it. He also asserted that I had not moved to collect twenty million dollars in back taxes owed by the Bank of Nevada . . . this was a very complicated matter having to do with whether you taxed the accounts or the stock. He brought suit against both me and the bank. Then I was sued by George Ullom, a Springer supporter, who said he had delivered the $100,000, and that Springer was not lying about it. Then Ullom sued me for $200,000 for defamation of character. [laughter] Then Springer said that I couldn't defeat Laxalt because of a credibility gap — that people did not believe my administration anymore. Towards the end of the primary he even charged that I was involved in a deal to under-value property at Lake Tahoe.

Springer's attack was a good one: not a word was true. In fact, his allegations were unbelievably silly. As governor I had nothing to do with setting or collecting taxes — nothing whatsoever — and I had nothing to do with property valu-ations. Those were the responsibilities of constitutional offices. As for the $100,000, that was something of which I had absolutely no knowledge. I thought, "Well, anybody who knows anything about how politics and government work will understand that these charges are specious, and will forget them." But that's not the way it played out — people tend to believe what they read in the newspapers. Of course, the big lawsuit that Ullom brought against me was dropped as soon as the primary was over, as I was sure it would be, because there was just no substance to it. But you don't need substance when you get into a campaign — you can make any charge you want to. And that's what Charlie Springer did.

I had made Springer my acting attorney general, and I had appointed Ullom to the Tax Commission and the Public Service Commission; and as far as I knew, Springer, Ullom, and Sawyer were all on the same team. Maybe there was a defect in my makeup, some sort of political myopia, because this sort of thing happened to me occasionally: People would come up and say, "Boy, I will never vote for you again as long as I live!"

"Why not?"

"Well, because you did so-and-so, and I'll never forgive you."

I would have no idea what they were talking about . . . some ruling that the Fish and Game Commission had made or something, and they were my sworn enemy for life! But this thing with Springer and Ullom went a little beyond that. Here were two people who had received appointments to major positions from me. You wonder — "I'm such a nice guy; how could Charlie do something like this to me? I thought that our relationship was a good one?" You get introspective and think you must be doing something wrong or this wouldn't be happening.

But that was not the case with Ted Marshall, whom I barely knew and who was no concern of mine. In 1962 Marshall, who was elected district attorney of Clark County as I won reelection to the governor's office, decided he had been slighted because I had not called him after my victory! [laughter] You just ride along and think everything is lovey-dovey, and you don't realize that people are sitting back resentful of something that you don't even know you did. Maybe I hadn't called him; probably I hadn't. A better politician probably would have. But I had no idea . . . . And in 1966 he too decided to oppose me in the primary.

I easily defeated Springer and Marshall in the Democratic primary, but Nevada newspapers dubbed the general election that followed "the battle of the century." Paul Laxalt was a very effective campaigner, and he had a unified party behind him, and the *Las Vegas Sun* was roasting me daily — had been for two or three years.

As in most political contests, the outcome would hinge on more than a single issue, but in 1966 even the propriety of my candidacy was questioned. George Abbott, chairman of the state Republicans, dug up newspaper reports of some of the speeches I had made when I was running against Russell in 1958, and quoted me: "Eight years is enough! No one is indispensable." It was true; I had said that . . . . Well, what I actually said was that eight years was enough for Charlie Russell. [laughter] But tradition is very difficult to overcome, and this was a big issue. No one had ever been elected to three terms; historically, two was sort of an accepted limit.

During the campaign I kept up my criticism of the federal government's Nazi tactics in Nevada, where the FBI under J. Edgar Hoover was violating both federal and state laws. I was one of the few people — maybe the only person in the United States — who was making this point, and I was making it not just in Nevada, but in speeches around the country. And contrary to certain politically-motivated allegations, I was not trying to protect casino gaming interests by going after Hoover: I was concerned about the FBI's invasion of the privacy of the citizens of this country, gaming people and non-gaming people alike. Hoover had spent years polishing his heroic law-and-order image, but he was apparently contemptuous of the Constitution, and he was relentless in his abuse of federal power.

I wasn't afraid to use the term "Nazi tactics" to describe what Hoover and the FBI were doing — that just about described the way I felt. But Paul Laxalt clearly sided with Hoover. He understood that J. Edgar was a folk hero, and that anyone attacking him was vulnerable politically; and near the end of the campaign (impeccable political timing) he sent Hoover a telegram apologizing for my behavior, releasing a copy to the press even before Hoover received it. Laxalt said he was "dismayed and ashamed . . . . " Then, just before the election (the whole thing was worked out pretty carefully), Hoover wrote a letter to Hank Greenspun of the *Las Vegas Sun,* which essentially said, "Don't reelect Grant Sawyer!" He also wrote that gaming was involved with organized crime — which it may have been to some extent, but that didn't give Hoover a license to violate the laws of the United States and the laws of Nevada. Nonetheless, the text of his letter appeared on the front page of the *Sun* in bold print, as I recall.

All this attention was a little flattering because it was the first time anybody could recall J. Edgar Hoover overtly intervening or using his position and prestige in a political campaign. Here was this great man taking the time to come down off his pedestal and meddle in an election in the state of Nevada, a fly speck on the map of American politics. And so eager to get rid of me! After trying for so long, I had finally gotten a response from Hoover. But of course, he hadn't sent it to me. [laughter]

During the campaign Laxalt attacked my gaming control policy; but the fact remains that any reform in the area of gaming control was made by me, and Laxalt's alleged concern seemed to disappear the day he was elected. He didn't try to change the structure at all; he just appointed his own people to it. That's politics.

Paul also had banners made up claiming that he was going to be the "lighthouse for education." In the year of the election 69 percent of Nevada's total budget was going for education, yet he accused me of not doing enough in that field . . . which was ironic, because if I had done a good job in any area, I had done an excellent job in education.[1] But I found out that teachers, like many other groups, are somewhat fickle, and if the Pied Piper comes along, it isn't what you did for me yesterday, it's what you are going to do for me tomorrow. I think I lost a lot of votes to my opponent's super-extravagant promises, such as community colleges for every county and city.

Other issues were even more damaging. The economy worked against me — nationally it was slowing down, and Clark County was suffering because of declines in tourism and in the patronage of gaming casinos. It's a truism of politics that in a community that's hurting economically, anybody in office is going to have difficulty being reelected, regardless of partisan politics or anything else, and in the general election I carried heavily-Democratic Clark County by only 651 votes. Civil rights may also have been an election factor. A couple of years earlier, at the Stardust Hotel before three hundred cheering Republicans, Laxalt had claimed that Kennedy's civil rights bill was unconstitutional, and that the real group that needed protection was businessmen, not minorities. [laughter] But I thought that battle had been kind of won by 1966 — most people understood they had to get with the program. Those who had resisted so fiercely, of course, still felt that they were justified in their resistance, and that I was a communist liberal running around loose who had to be stopped.

About a month before the general I knew that I was not going to win, and I told a number of people that. You can sense these things if you are at all objective — campaigning, seeing hundreds of people every day, you develop a sense of how you are being received, and I was getting a negative reaction from too many people. A governor never really makes any new friends: at the start everybody is your friend, but every day, by purpose or by accident, you make somebody mad, and it has a cumulative effect — eventually your enemies outnumber your friends. With the gaming industry in particular, enemies once made are always there, and we had revoked some licenses in addition to Sinatra's, including one at the Desert Inn. I lost a lot of votes right there — all the D.I. people and their families, relatives, and friends. Gaming in general went strongly for Laxalt, but those things happened in every area, not just in gaming. Also, Mr. Springer had inflicted considerable damage on me in the primary, maybe enough to sink me in the general election . . . I don't know, but a three-thousand-vote swing in that general would have been the difference. As governor, I had made a lot of decisions and taken action on a lot of issues, so it was natural that eventually time and friends were going to run out . . . and in 1966 mine did. I lost.[2]

Part Three

_____

players and issues,
public and private

11

lionel sawyer & collins

I was physically, emotionally and mentally exhausted when the 1966 campaign was over, and I had not the slightest desire ever to rerun that particular movie. With my defeat, the black day had come when the Sawyers would no longer be feeding from the public trough. [laughter] President Johnson offered to appoint me governor of the Canal Zone, but it would have been silly to accept. In Panama I'd have relatively limited authority and power, and as soon as the next presidential election came along someone else would be appointed and I would be asking the same question as before: "What am I going to do?" In fact, although I didn't know it at the time, I would not accept any of the several opportunities to hold public office that would later come my way. Henceforth I would concentrate on a law career that had been subordinate to politics since I was elected district attorney of Elko County fifteen years before.

I began looking for a partnership in a firm with top flight lawyers, because I had little confidence in my ability to practice law on my own. (I didn't even know how to file a paper at the courthouse.) Judge Zenoff, whom I had appointed to the Nevada supreme court, suggested that I go down to Las Vegas and talk to Sam Lionel, who was considered by many to be the best lawyer in the state. Sam and his only associate, Bob Buckalew (still with the firm), had an office in the First National Bank building. It wasn't a big firm with a structured practice, and it looked like the sort of thing that would be right for me because I wanted to be in a position to learn quickly how to practice law. After meeting with Sam Lionel I was convinced that he was the person to teach me. So Sam and I formed a partnership in February, 1967.

Even as I was resuming private practice, an old political connection came into play. The Education Commission of the States, with funding from a number of states (Nevada not among them), does studies and makes reports on issues of concern to its members. The then chairman of the National Governors' Conference, which controlled the commission, was a friend of mine, and he offered me the position of national counsel for the commission. I accepted. I didn't have high regard for the commission, which appeared to be just another of these groups whose staff is dedicated to self-perpetuation, but the annual pay was thirty thousand dollars, which was more than I had been receiving as governor of Nevada! And my duties were slight. Once a month I went to the Denver headquarters, and occasionally I had to attend a conference of some kind, but there wasn't much else required of me except that I answer legal questions when they arose. I did that for a couple of years, and it was a big bonanza for the firm. Sam might correct me on this, but I believe that in those early years our total annual income was around sixty thousand dollars, half of which I was bringing in as national counsel for the Education Commission of the States.

Indirectly, Paul Laxalt created a far more important source of income for the firm by insisting that corporate gaming operations be licensed in the state of Nevada. (Although many people give *me* credit for it, I had always resisted this.) Corporate gaming became legal in 1969, and as a consequence most of the resort hotel-casinos in Las Vegas were bought out by corporations . . . nearly all of whom came to me to take care of their licensing. This became a *tremendous* source of business for our firm. If you handled the licensing of a new owner, in all probability you would continue to represent that entity in all of its other legal matters; and over three or four years I picked up most of the licensing of new corporate ownerships in Las Vegas, in turn generating business for the other areas of our practice. Why so many chose our firm to represent them remains a mystery to me. Probably the perception was that since I'd been governor for eight years and knew something about gaming regulation, I was the guy to come to. It must not have concerned them that Governor Laxalt was my political adversary; and in truth I was treated with considerable courtesy by Laxalt's administration and by the others that followed, Republican and Democrat alike.

The Corporate Gaming Act of 1969 provided the initial impetus for our firm's startling growth, and gaming law continues to be one of our specialties. We still represent most of the corporations that I originally licensed, and since that time there have been a number of other changes in ownership, one corporation selling a property to another and so on. Gaming put a lot of flesh on the bones of the young Lionel-Sawyer law firm, but Sam was a top litigator (still is) who

already had a very healthy commercial practice with devel-
opers and others, and we also built on that. The new gaming
business merged nicely with Sam's established practice, and
combined they remain the backbone of our practice to this
day.

As our firm grew, we
took on additional partners and associates; and we have
always been careful in our selections. In order to be a good
lawyer, you must have a sensitivity to people so that you can
understand not only where your client is coming from, but
also the other side; and you ought to have some street sense,
and be interested in things that make the community, the
state and the nation. If you're just a lawyer who sits in the
office and does nothing but prepare motions and briefs and
that sort of thing, you won't be good in the courtroom where
you have to evaluate a jury; and if you don't have any
interests, any passions, outside of just sitting and practicing
law, you're not going to be a very well-rounded person.

You could fill a law firm with bright and able people, but
if they're so narrow that they don't understand the world
they're living in, you're going to wind up with a bunch of
clerks, which is not what the practice of law is all about. So
when I interview young attorneys who are applying for jobs
at Lionel Sawyer & Collins, I ask about their lives outside the
profession. What were their activities in law school and in
undergraduate school? Were they active in organizations?
What are their personal interests beyond the practice of law?
I don't care what their political affiliation is or even how they
view social issues; in fact I really don't care what it is they're
interested in. Are they interested in *something*, that's what I
want to know . . . if I can find it out without violating all the
laws of interviewing and getting sued. [laughter]

Jon Collins was a navy veteran of World War II, and a friend from my law school days at Georgetown. We both returned to Nevada after getting our law degrees — me to Elko and Jon to Ely, his hometown. While I was district attorney in Elko, Jon was elected to the same office in White Pine County, and in 1958 he won the race for district court judge in the same general election that put me in the governor's mansion. When a vacancy occurred on the Nevada supreme court, I appointed Jon to fill it. He continued on the bench after my 1966 defeat, but he had rather a large family, and you just don't make that much money in public service. Sitting next to him on a flight one day I asked if he would like to join our firm . . . earn a lot more money. Indeed, he would. Jon resigned from the supreme court, and the firm became Lionel Sawyer & Collins.

Robert D. Faiss, a city editor for the *Las Vegas Sun*, was a good friend of Dick Ham, who was with me from the beginning of my political career. After I was elected governor Dick brought Bob to Carson City, and he went to work for the Nevada Gaming Commission when we changed the structure of gaming enforcement. One of the earliest things Bob did was write the first "how-to" book on Nevada gaming — a summary of all of the statutes and regulations combined with instructions for applicants, who could pick it up and know that this was how you proceeded to get a license. Bob turned out to be an absolutely phenomenal writer.

Eventually Bob moved over to the governor's office as my executive assistant, in which role he took care of making sure that my speeches indicated that I knew what I was talking about. [laughter] If I was asked to speak about subject x, for example, Bob would go to the proper division of state government and say, "The governor has to give a speech on x on such-and-such a date. Would you please send me something suitable on that subject." The agency would draft a speech on the subject and send it in, and Bob would rewrite the ones that were not particularly competent. That went on all the time, because I was giving a speech a day. In fact, one year we figured I gave more speeches than there were days! [laughter] So I had to have a constant flow of material on an array of subjects. Eventually, Bob was handling the whole thing. He became very familiar with my style, and most of what I wrote or said for the last several years of my governorship came out of Bob Faiss, who would rewrite it and was the final arbiter on all of those things.

After I left the governor's office Bob went to Washington, where he ultimately wound up in the White House as Lyndon Johnson's deputy appointments secretary. He also was a principal advance person for the president. In this capacity he would travel to a destination several days before the president to see that arrangements were in order. At the White House, Bob would be in charge of setting up situations, such as seeing that proper protocol was followed for a visit from the ambassador from Ghana, for example. He had an office in the White House, and his association with the president was a very close and very good one. He has hanging on his wall a picture of Lyndon Johnson in which Johnson is thanking him for his services.

All the while, Bob was going to law school at night, and just as soon as he got his law degree he returned to Las Vegas and joined us at Lionel Sawyer & Collins. I would say that he is now the preeminent gaming law attorney in the nation. He has helped produce many books and countless articles, and he helped start the International Association of Gaming Attorneys and served as one of its first presidents. Bob represents the Nevada Resort Association and a number of prominent resort-hotels on gaming matters, and he has been invited on several occasions to go to other states and other countries to help set up their gaming regulations and statutes.

I appointed Bert Goldwater to be a member of the first Nevada Gaming Commission. Bert was from an old Jewish family in Reno, and he had attended the University of Nevada, as had his brother, David, who lives in Las Vegas now, and his sister, Nonie. They were all Nevadans in every sense of the word. When I appointed him I didn't even know whether Bert was a Democrat or a Republican, but I respected his convictions. He was socially sensitive and conscientious, and he displayed great courage in the positions he took, which were certainly not in conformance with either Reno or Las Vegas thinking at that time. Bert later became a member of the firm of Lionel Sawyer & Collins, and he has been a bankruptcy judge for many years. He is articulate, eloquent, and an excellent attorney — highly respected throughout the state.

We continue to have a big gaming practice, but there are other very able gaming firms in town; and although we still represent many of the resort hotel-casinos that I originally licensed over twenty years ago, there are a number of new people in town whom we do not represent. You can't represent everybody. From our original, somewhat narrow focus, we have evolved into a very diversified, full-service law firm. We have a large administrative practice and a full time lobby effort in the state legislature. Jeff Zucker, one of our partners who was trained by Sam Lionel, heads our big commercial department, which represents utilities and business people and so forth. We also have an emerging bankruptcy department with six or seven people in it, and we have some specialists in hospitals — we represent a number of hospitals throughout the state, including Humana in Las Vegas. We are developing labor expertise, as well, and we have five or six very bright young people in our growing environmental practice.

Lionel Sawyer & Collins started a newsletter to all of our gaming clients, and in the area of gaming law we have published five books — Tony Cabot, one of our partners, has been responsible for that effort. Attorneys from all over the world contributed chapters to our book on international gaming law (Tony was one of the editors), and eight or nine lawyers in our firm wrote the part on how to obtain a gaming license in Nevada. That stuff is all good and very productive. It's like the trips we used to take to persuade industry to come to Nevada: "You can't say we got a client because of this book, but you don't know."

A couple of weeks ago someone called from Mexico. Mexico was going to change its laws on gaming, and he wanted to start a resort area there and have us come down and represent him. I said, "Why would you want me to come to Mexico to represent you before Mexican authorities?"

He said, "Because I read your book!" So you just don't know the effect these things have.

What's happened to the firm has been beyond my wildest expectations — I never dreamed that things would go this well, and I couldn't have asked for a better association than the one I have had with our members all these years . . . particularly Sam Lionel. Sam is a studious lawyer's lawyer who is greatly respected throughout the bar. His reputation extends far beyond Nevada. Sam was recently appointed to an advisory group for the Appellate Court of the Ninth Judicial Circuit, and he served for many years as chairman of the Committee on Bar Admittance.

Our personal relationship has been quite good, even though Sam and I are very different people. As its senior partners, it's important to the whole firm that the two of us get along. Sam knows a lot more about business law and some other fields of our firm's practice than I do, and I generally defer to his judgment on those subjects, but I am a little more assertive with respect to community and state affairs — most of the time we simply agree on things. Our partnership has been extremely gratifying. I have been lucky all my life, of course, and I was particularly lucky the day twenty-five years ago when the two of us alone decided to start this firm.

We have come a long way from our modest beginnings: we now occupy three floors of the bank building in Las Vegas, and we have a branch of the firm in Reno. Although the size of our staff fluctuates a little, we employ somewhere around sixty lawyers in Las Vegas, and fifteen or sixteen in Reno. We are the largest law firm in Las Vegas, and probably the second largest in Reno; and combined, Lionel Sawyer & Collins is now the largest law firm in Nevada.

12

politics and the family

My father was the only doctor in Fallon. I don't know whether he was a good doctor or not, but he had a hell of a bedside manner; he probably cured more people mentally than he did physically. [laughter] Apparently, Dad *was* a good doctor, and he had a reputation for being a particularly good diagnostician. He would diagnose and then send the patients to Reno or San Francisco for treatment, and he was nearly always right.

Dad had a real instinct for medicine . . . but I think his first love was politics. He was really a prominent citizen in Fallon, and for many years he was *the* Democrat there. When James Scrugham would run, he would come to Fallon to consult with my father; McCarran also stopped there during a few years, at least until they got into a big feud . . . . All of the politicos would stop to see my father. Of course, places like Fallon and Elko were then a great deal more important politically than they are today. There was a political kingpin in each town, and you had to call on him if you were on the campaign trail; if you didn't, you'd make a bitter enemy, because they all had big egos.

My dad would organize Fallon for a particular candidate: the word would come down from him, "This year we're going to be for McCarran," and they would have meetings and do all the things you do in a political campaign, and then it was up to him to deliver the votes. My father attended all of the state Democratic conventions, and he had to have been considered a really big wheel back then, when Nevada's little counties amounted to something politically.

A couple of times my father decided that he would run for governor. He would summon all of his political cohorts from throughout the state to the only hotel in Hazen, a very small town some distance outside of Fallon. There they'd gather to plan his campaign, and there they'd get drunk and stay drunk for three or four days. [laughter] Then the campaign would end, and Dad would come back to Fallon. That's as far as he ever got down the road to the governor's mansion. He did, however, spend two consecutive terms (1935-1939) representing Churchill County in the state senate, and he did some good things there, authoring and passing the first public health law in the state, and pushing the creation of Nevada's first drug and alcohol department. I would go over to the capitol when I was in college, and he would take me around and introduce me to the legislators and include me in what was going on.

Later, my father served on the parole board of the state prison for eight years, appointed by Charlie Russell, who was governor before me. Dad's term expired a couple of days before I was sworn in as governor, and obviously I could not appoint my own father; but gentleman that Governor Russell was, he reappointed Dad before leaving office. Charlie and I had just gone through a bitter campaign, and I am sure he had no use for me whatsoever, but he did that, to my everlasting gratitude. It actually made me a little ashamed of some of the things that I had said about him during the campaign. [laughter]

Although Dad was considered a liberal Democrat, certainly he was not one in the sense that we use the term today. He didn't like Orientals; he didn't care for blacks; he just had no tolerance for anybody who was different from us, whether by color, background, or ethnicity. It was even alleged that he was a member of the Ku Klux Klan. (When I grew politically active in Nevada that story became rather prominent.) But he was a perfectly charming, fascinating man, and after I got to know him better I discounted some of the stories that I had heard about him, and decided that he was simply an unusual person.

My father's racist, protectionist, discriminatory, and elitist views were not unconventional for his time. (They were shared by my wife's father.) His attitudes may have derived in part from his puritan background, which was very different from my mother's — in those days, the Protestants hated the Catholics, the Mormons, and the Jews. Interestingly, although my mother and I believed very differently from him, Dad wasn't particularly intolerant of us having our positions, and he didn't attempt to influence me. I think he figured that it wouldn't make any difference. [laughter] And perhaps he believed that I was a little frivolous and silly — that I was sort of a dreamer who would eventually grow up and understand how things really worked. Anyway, he didn't make a big point of it, and we never argued about our differences on the issues of racial and social equality.

During the years that the Wingfield group ran Nevada, Dad opposed them. He thought Wingfield's banks had too much power, so he campaigned against the banking interests when he ran for the senate. (My father was much like a lot of people: against any conspiracy that he ain't in. [laughter] And he wasn't in that one, so he campaigned against it.) I suspect that he was against any group that he thought had too much control, although he was very partial to railroads since he was a railroad doctor. As a matter of fact, he introduced bills when he was in the legislature that were pro-railroad, and he was sort of considered their spokesman. Apparently the control issue didn't apply to railroads. [laughter]

Dad didn't always follow the party line, by any means — he sort of revelled in being different and setting his own course on things, and he and McCarran fell out bitterly after he'd been part of the McCarran group for several years. Whatever it was about, it was very bad, and for the rest of their lives I doubt that they spoke to one another again . . . but right up to his death, Dad was considered one of the bigwigs of the Democratic party. He really knew Nevada politicians and Nevada issues, and he was of tremendous help to me when I entered politics as a relative newcomer to the state. Of course, my father had always wanted to be governor, and I suspect that he vicariously satisfied that ambition through my election. He attended all of the affairs that I had when I was governor, and he sat in the front row, and was in the receiving line, and all that stuff . . . he just loved it.

My brother Harry graduated from high school and went on to Linfield College, which was then a small Baptist school in McMinnville, Oregon. After two years at Linfield he transferred to the University of Nevada, where he got his degree. He then went on to medical school, graduated about the time World War II started, and went into the service as a medical doctor. During the war Harry was in the European theater, and after the war he went back to San Francisco and resumed his practice in obstetrics-gynecology. He married a girl from Fallon named Elizabeth Best, whom he had met at the University of Nevada, and they had two children, one of whom, Thomas Sawyer, is on the faculty at the University of Nevada, Reno. The other, a daughter named Laeta, lives in California.

My brother Milo Cameron Sawyer was a little different from my brother Harry, in that he was very much interested in the arts. He had my father's gorgeous voice, was an excellent speaker and debater, and participated in dramatics in high school and in college. Milo also went to Linfield College, but he was far more religiously oriented than either my older brother or I, and after graduating he entered the seminary at Colgate, in Hamilton, New York. Following graduation from the seminary, he became a Baptist minister and wound up in Toledo, Ohio, as minister of the First Baptist Church.

Milo soon became a leader among liberal Baptists, and he spent most of his life fighting the Southern Baptists, who are similar to Holy Rollers — as a general rule they interpret the Bible strictly. My brother was very concerned about the poor and all of the social issues of the day, and he was more academic and philosophical in his approach to religion than the Southern Baptists. As a matter of fact, he was almost fired as pastor of the church in Toledo because he had the temerity to tell the Board of Deacons that he really didn't care whether Mary was a virgin or not; it had nothing to do with his concept of religion. That was so scandalous that they had a big hearing, but he kept his job. Milo was a very interesting fellow, and I think he would have had a great future within the church at the national level, but he died of stomach cancer in his early thirties. He had three sons, all of whom still survive.

After I went off to college my mother became the matron of the mental institution in Blackfoot, Idaho, a position she held for a number of years. Later she took the same kind of job in an institution in Connecticut, where she worked until she deteriorated mentally and emotionally to the point where she couldn't sustain herself at all. I brought her back to Elko, where I had started a law practice, but it became necessary to put her in a rest home. Since there were none in Elko, I had the very onerous job of driving her to Salt Lake City and putting her in a home there. My aunt Fern was with me or we would never have made it, because my mother was getting more and more aggressive and physical. She was extremely abusive, and she kept trying to jerk the car off the road; it was just terrible! For the few remaining years of her life I would get calls from Salt Lake that she was in the police station claiming I had abandoned her and so on. By then I was district attorney of Elko County, and these calls were pretty embarrassing.

My mother spent the remaining three or four years of her life in several different rest homes — she'd go in one and raise so much hell that they would call and say, "You've got to take her out of here!" This was a very trying time for me; it was terrible because my relationship with her during the early years had been so close. I really sort of idolized my mother, and then to have to deal with her in that fashion just about killed me. My brother Milo had died by then, and Harry was in San Francisco, too far away to help. (He did help with the finances, however, paying half the cost of keeping her in the homes.)

My mother's sister Fern was an important person in my life. She was very much like my mother, but certainly a good deal more stable in her later years, and as she saw what was happening to my mother she was quite protective of me. I adored Aunt Fern from the time I was born, and I was close to her children, and even their children now. She was very outgoing, very personable, and very nice looking.

Aunt Fern was a teacher all of her life, winding up as a librarian in the Boise school system. She was a pleasant, fair person who did not go the same route physically and mentally as my mother: she was still in pretty good shape when she died, and she must have been close to eighty. Aunt Fern was a died-in-the-wool Democrat, quite active in politics, and during my years as Nevada's governor I would get her together with Idaho governors and other politicians, which she really liked.

When Senator Bible decided not to seek reelection in 1974, I was one of the first people he informed, along with Mike O'Callaghan. Not that he was encouraging me to run for his vacant seat — he just said, "I want to let you know." That would have been an opportunity, and the polls looked good, but by then I didn't much desire public office anymore. My law practice was coming along well, and I knew that life in Washington was no bed of roses. There you're just one among a lot of people, and unless you distinguish yourself, cut yourself from the pack — which takes many years to do — you may not gain much gratification. Plus, I understood what it was like to be in the public eye, on stage all the time, with people checking your every move. By then I had had eight years of freedom from that, and I loved it; I didn't want to dive back into the fishbowl and live from one election to another the rest of my life. And I couldn't face the idea of going into a heavy campaign, begging for money and doing all the onerous things you must do to get there and stay there in politics. Bette wouldn't have stood for it anyway: she was quoted as saying, "If he files, I'll file!" [laughter] I didn't run, and that was the end. I have never even considered running for public office since.

Bette was always uncomfortable with the superficiality and artificiality of the political game, but throughout our marriage she has been for me a pillar of strength, loyalty, and restraint. For close to fifty years now she has curbed my inclination to excess, and kept me from disaster with her solid, no-non-sense, dead-honest analysis of my proclivities. Bette is a person of such integrity that many who detest me, think very highly of her.

Our daughter, Gail, is an interesting, attractive person completely without guile, who has been the one constant joy of our lives since her birth. Gail was born in 1949 in Elko, and she was nine when I was elected governor and we moved to Carson City. Being uprooted in the third or fourth grade and moved to a new town with a totally different ambience . . . the experience was pretty traumatic. Even though I had been district attorney in Elko, we had not been public figures to the extent that there was any great pressure on us, but when we got to Carson City we were suddenly in the "big time" and under everybody's scrutiny. It was a completely different thing, and the politics of the situation made it even more difficult.

Carson City was a conservative, Republican-oriented town, and we were Democrats dispossessing a respected Republican governor whose family was well liked. Charlie Russell's wife, daughter of the popular Judge Clark Guild, had been born

Gail, Bette, and Grant on the campaign trail, 1962

"Bette was always uncomfortable with the superficiality and artificiality of the political game . . . and Gail was never one to join the club except when she felt she had to when I was running."

and reared in Carson City, and some of his children were close to Gail's age. As a consequence we encountered a lot of hostility, some of it directed at Gail at school, even from her teachers. I felt awfully sorry for her. She was unfairly bearing the burden of my victory, and although she took it pretty well, she was determined not to get into any difficulty or impose any of her problems on me or Bette. As a consequence, she didn't have the normal give and take of childhood. Other kids could run around and do all these juvenile things, but she felt she couldn't.

It was made more difficult for Gail because we were living in a house which not only didn't belong to us, but was actually sort of a public monument. She could have friends over, but I don't think she ever felt right about it: she never knew if they were there because they liked her or because they wanted to come to the mansion. So Gail developed an early and rather unfortunate caution about her personal relationships, which wasn't good, particularly for an only child. (If she had had two or three brothers or sisters, and they all had been able to share their problems with one another, I think it would have been easier.)

Gail had to grow up awfully fast — much faster than she probably should have — and the press was on her all the time, too: "What do you think of this? What do you think of the eighteen-year-old vote? Who is your favorite for president?" We never put any pressure on her to conform to our positions, and although she was cautious about the press, she would occasionally take a position contrary to one that I had expressed publicly. For example, she was opposed to the eighteen-year-old vote, and I was very much for it. The press had a lot of fun with that. And her choices for president and other offices were not always the same as mine.

Gail developed a sort of independence, perhaps because she just didn't want to be totally stifled. She got tired of being a Sawyer during those years, always on stage with very little privacy, and when she graduated from high school she didn't stay in Nevada — she went away to college, I think to get out on her own and away from these pressures. After a year and a half at Colorado Women's College in Denver, she spent a year on a college cruise ship that went all around the world. It was a marvelous experience for her. Then she transferred to Arizona State University, where she got her degree.

Once one of Gail's roommates came home for Christmas with her, and was roaming around our house looking at pictures, and said, "Gail, what are all these pictures of your father with presidents?"

Gail said, "Well, he was governor of Nevada when those were taken." The girl had never been told.

To this day, Gail doesn't identify herself as the daughter of a former governor unless people ask. I can understand that. Even after she graduated from Arizona State with a master's degree in education, she didn't come to Nevada to teach; she went to Pennsylvania. (Eventually, she did come back and taught for several years.) Being the governor's daughter was a heavy burden for Gail. I feel for young children who get into this game at an early age: unless their parents are extremely wise, it can be very difficult for them.

On the plus side we often took Gail with us when traveling on state business, and she got to meet all of the major players in American politics. She became friends with Hubert Humphrey and Jack Kennedy, and, of course, she met many of the nation's governors. But there were certain trips we couldn't take her on, such as one to South America with a group of governors for three weeks, and one to Japan with another group as a representative for President Kennedy. (I don't think there were even wives on that trip.) There were a number of trips that Gail couldn't go on, but she did see much of the world during those years.

Gail and I had relatively little time together from the day we moved to Carson City until after I had finished my two terms as governor. I was on a full schedule all the time. Every morning I would wake up and I would have the schedule for the day in front of me, and I followed that. And at night, we were seldom home. Bette made time to be there for Gail when she left for school and when she came home in the afternoon, but I couldn't do that . . . but today I have a very good relationship with her. She's a marvelous person, extremely sensitive to the family, and I adore her. She doesn't make a host of friends; that isn't her bag. But she has very close friends, more than most people have, and she's had them for years — interesting friends with whom she corresponds, like teachers and other people who are not in the political world at all. In fact, Gail's quite non-political.

Gail is extremely close to her mother; they've always been best friends. The two of them are much more conservative in most areas than I am, and we still disagree on a lot of public issues. She's a Democrat, but she was never one to join the club except when she felt she had to when I was running — she would be in the Young Democrats and the Gals for Grant and those things. But those were all part of my world, not a political world as far as she was concerned, and she's never aspired to do anything in a formal political party sense.

13

"never run against
a democrat who is
doing a good job"

In the old days a person who wanted to have some influence in state party affairs could do so, and, at the same time, exert a measure of influence on national policy. You simply registered as a Democrat and attended precinct meetings when they were called. Then you ran to be elected a delegate to the county meeting; and at the county convention, you ran to be elected a delegate to the state convention. (Each county was entitled to x number of delegates.) In presidential years you campaigned to be elected a delegate to the national convention. There was no great mystery to it, except that you had to be active and attend the meetings. It wasn't that difficult, and that was the way political machines were built.

In Nevada, Pat McCarran was very concerned with every precinct election. He had to control everything — each county had to be his; each delegate had to be his. Everybody associated with the Democratic operation had to be a McCarran person, and he spent a lot of time controlling that from the bottom up. He had his people at each precinct and at each county and state convention, because he wanted to be a big wheel nationally . . . and he was. He wanted his people, and only his people, to be delegates to the national convention so he could say to Harry Truman, or whoever it was, "I will deliver you twenty votes from Nevada."

By contrast, after McCarran's death Alan Bible stayed out of precinct and county politics. Many people felt that he should have assumed more leadership than he did after McCarran's death, and not let the state Democratic party flounder and go its own way. But it was Bible's philosophy that you gained nothing by getting involved in these intra-party fights — who's going to be the master of ceremonies, and so forth. He sort of rode on top of the whole process, and he did so quite successfully. Alan Bible wanted everybody to love him . . . and they did, as a rule.

It's important that the party be solidly behind its candidate. You want its leaders not necessarily to be your people, but to be people who will support you — who will applaud at the right times, and who will say the right things. If your administration gets into trouble, you don't want a lot of back-biting from the party leadership, and you won't get it if they're your people or on your team. When I was governor I was proactive in party affairs: I wanted to know that the chairman of a county's Democratic party was a Sawyer man, which wasn't always the case. I wanted the people who controlled the party apparatus to be for me, and we had some knock-down-drag-outs, particularly after I was first elected. Nevada's Democratic national committeemen had supported my Republican opponent in the general election, and I felt that since they wouldn't support Democrats, and particularly since they hadn't supported *me*, they had to go. [laughter] So at the Ely state convention we had a big purge of the party, and we defeated them all.

Being a party leader used to be a big deal, and everybody knew who they were, but about the only time you see their names in the paper now is when they're fighting over who's going to be at the head table or something. [laughter] I was the Democratic national committeeman from Nevada for twenty years after I left office. Elected to the committee in 1968, I served through 1988 when I decided not to run again. Under the system employed when I came up the committee cared about what I thought, because I had as many votes as each member did, and more influence than most. But as soon as we got one-man-one-vote in party affairs, small states (Nevada and others) lost every shred of influence in the party. We'd meet maybe two or three times a year, and I'd see my buddies, have a few cocktails, and tell old stories. But that was about all — nobody really cared what Nevada thought about anything, and in the ensuing years we became less and less influential in national affairs.

Parties have deteriorated in the last ten years to the point where they are now virtually irrelevant. They spend most of their time arguing about who's going to sit at the head table and who's going to chair this committee or that one — nothing of any consequence. You can put a lot of time and energy into this daily scuffle, scrambling for a position that is totally meaningless after you get it, and that's what parties pretty much do on both sides now. As formal political structures, they don't amount to much.

While I was governor there had been frequent talk that I would run against Howard Cannon for the U.S. Senate . . . it kept the staff stirred up.

[laughter] And Walter Baring was always scared to death that I was going to run against him, so we had staff becoming suspicious of one another, and spreading rumors, and that sort of thing. The press was constantly speculating that I would run against somebody for some national office, but my position had always been that I would never run against a Democrat who was doing a good job . . . and I felt that way about Cannon.

Howard Cannon had been elected to the United States Senate the year that I was elected governor, but we didn't know one another. I had lived in the north all my life, and except for Democratic party matters had had little contact with Las Vegas, which was his home. My good friend Fred Anderson, a Reno surgeon, was defeated by Cannon in the primary, and after the primary Cannon and I campaigned together throughout the state, as did all of the Democratic nominees for state offices. As a United States senator, Cannon proved to be able and sincere, and he quickly became an influential member of senate committees whose decisions affected Nevada. By the time he left office, I was convinced that he was one of the better senators in the history of our state.

As governor, I had fairly frequent meetings and telephone conferences with Nevada's Senators Cannon and Bible, and to a lesser extent with Congressman Baring. Cannon had a good office staff modeled somewhat after Senator McCarran's, and he responded quickly to constituent requests. But if he could not do anything for you, he didn't try to kid you. He would say, "I will look into this and do my best; but I don't think it can be done, and I'll tell you why." He was candid and forthright about those things, and I found him to be the same in his personal affairs. Howard Cannon wouldn't try to con you.

Howard was a little more liberal than Alan Bible, who was moderate to conservative and most of the time in the conservative camp. While Bible felt that he was representing his constituents in Nevada, Cannon may have been a little bit out in front of his on social and civil rights matters. There were a great many things about Howard that I admired, but I was personally closer to Alan, perhaps because he and I had a shared background — he was from Fallon, where my father was a doctor for forty years, and we were both McCarran Boys who pretty much talked the same language. I considered Alan Bible a good personal friend.

There was little phony pretense about Alan . . . some, but not a lot; he didn't parade as much as many senators do. But he was a consummate politician — he would make it a point to sit down and talk with his "old friend," the editor, any time he came to a town, and every newspaper in the state was for him. He was also highly respected in the Senate, where he was a strong protector of Nevada's interests as chairman of an Interior subcommittee and as a member of the appropriations committee.

When Alan Bible was attorney general of Nevada before he ran for the Senate, Bob McDonald was a deputy attorney general. Bob was a good Democrat whose father was the editor of the *Nevada State Journal*, and he was moving pretty fast in those years. When Bible left the attorney general's office for private practice, he took one client with him: the Colorado River Commission . . . and he brought along his old deputy, Bob McDonald, to be his partner. So the firm of Bible & McDonald started with one client, but it was a client that kept them afloat for a while. Then Alan ran for the United States Senate and won, and the law office was *still* called Bible & McDonald. (In those days a senator could leave his name on his firm.) Alan's name later had to come off, so Bob brought Alan's son into the firm and retained the Bible name on the shingle.

Bob McDonald was Bible's friend and protector, and probably closer to him politically and personally than anyone else. They were an interesting match. Bob is free-thinking, free-swinging, and Alan Bible was anything but; he was, I think, in McDonald's terms, "the square of all squares." [laughter] Bob was a colorful, witty guy. We were about the same age, and we got to know each other as I came onto the political stage, and we have remained good friends ever since. Actually, Bob McDonald's been a friend and confidant of all the governors, both Republican and Democrat — they've all had confidence that they could ask him to do something, and he would do it. He was a tremendously effective fund raiser, and he is still sort of the grandfather of politics in Reno. Of course, for many years he had Alan Bible's name to use, which was not to be sneezed at when it came to soliciting political contributions.

At the Democratic National Convention in 1960 Bible and Cannon were strong backers of Lyndon Johnson, and this caused some strain in our relationship . . . but nothing that lasted. When you're in this business — I shouldn't call it a business, but it is — you understand that sometimes as a matter of principle you have to take a different position from even your best friends and closest allies; and when you do that, you may occasionally be critical of them.

Now, Lyndon Johnson was the Senate leader, and he kept a firm grip on everything that was going on in the Senate. He passed out all the favors; he appointed people to committees . . . . The senators were Johnson's constituents, and he did all the things that you need to do to help a constituent, and they were very much aware that if they got on his wrong side they were in trouble. Bible and Cannon were responsive to this arrangement, particularly Bible: "The leader wants this, so I'll be part of the team and I'll help him." While I knew where they were coming from, I didn't have to follow Lyndon Johnson. Johnson wasn't *my* leader. I simply believed Kennedy would be a better president, and I hoped they understood that.

It got a little tense at the convention. We were fighting for the votes of the Nevada delegation, and Bible, Cannon and Baring were all on Johnson's side. Not that the outcome would mean a hell of a lot, but I wanted to be able to say to my man, "Look — Nevada supported you." There was a lot of scrambling around, and Alan, who usually wasn't that aggressive on these things, was really putting intense pressure on some delegates that I thought were mine. And when the senior senator calls you in and you are a delegate, he can put the fear of God in you! [laughter] So in the high political heat of the convention we had a little conversation back and forth about that; and for one of the few times that anybody can remember, Alan Bible became passionate and lost his temper and began yelling and doing some other very uncharacteristic things. He may even have been able to switch a couple of delegates' votes.[1] [laughter] So we had words. But nothing was said that was taken personally or dwelled on for any length of time . . . certainly not by me, and I don't believe by Alan and the others.

When Walter Baring was first elected to Congress in 1949 it was as a liberal, and I mean a *big* liberal. He took all the right positions on civil rights, and I was very pleased with his election; but as time went by he became more and more conservative, to the point where finally he could be considered one of the "boll weevils," the primarily southern congressmen who were opposed to nearly everything that I thought was progressive. He moved away from what I thought were the Democratic party's positions on most things, and our relationship deteriorated. We couldn't even agree on what was best for Nevada; in fact, I felt he frequently took positions that were *contrary* to the best interests of our state, and our relationship became so strained that I wouldn't meet with him unless Cannon or Bible was present. He was always perfectly polite to me, but I never knew whether he was going to go out and call a press conference and lambaste us all, or what he was going to do.

What a paradoxical politician Walter was! He was on the outs with Lyndon Johnson, who wouldn't even mention his name when referring to the Nevada delegation, but that was OK with Walter. Didn't bother him at all; he may even have gotten some votes out of it. And he must have had a refined sense of which way the political wind was blowing, because even when his colleagues in Congress passed him over for committee chairmanships it didn't bother him. Walter was consistently mercurial, fighting with everybody and out of step with everybody all the time, but he certainly was successful. He always got elected, and usually by huge majorities. Nobody liked him except the voters. [laughter]

Clearly, Walter knew what it took to be a successful politician — he was a congressman for almost thirty years. His greatest strengths were that he paid attention to every detail, and that he probably had the most efficient and attentive office staff of anyone who has ever served Nevada in Congress . . . . He did little things like send seed catalogs to all the ladies, catalogs which he got free from the government. Every year my mother would get a seed catalog from

Walter Baring. [laughter] And he kept close track of people's birthdays and sent them congratulations. He did everything. His attention to his constituents was unparalleled, but he never did anything particularly important for the state of Nevada in all the years that he was in Congress.

All the time that I was governor Ralph Denton was very active in national and state Democratic politics, and twice he ran against Walter Baring for Congress — an impossible undertaking, but he came close. I supported Ralph as much as I could, but a governor can't get too publicly involved in other races. If you are a prominent figure or an office holder, the rule of thumb is "May the best man win." You support the Democrat who takes the primary; that's the wise political position for an office holder, and it is general practice: presidents do it, titular heads of parties do it, and I felt bound by that custom.

There *are* certain ways you can be helpful without getting too involved, such as suggesting to your friends that they give their financial support, and being sure that at public events your candidate has a good spot and is not overlooked. You cannot, however, take any public position between two Democrats, and I didn't . . . although my differences with Walter Baring were generally known. I was pretty popular in some areas, and there I discreetly passed the word that "Denton is the guy we are for." There were other areas where I was not at all popular, and where I would not want to tout Ralph Denton; he would take on all my enemies. Sometimes you can do more damage than you do good.

Ralph Denton would have been an excellent congressman. I knew him about as well as I knew anybody, and I can tell you that he was a man of great character and honesty and conviction, and he wasn't afraid to state his positions and fight for them. Walter just didn't reflect what I thought a Democrat from Nevada should stand for, and Ralph did.

Ralph campaigned very hard against Walter Baring, and I think those races and losses took a lot out of him, financially and otherwise, because he hasn't been involved in party politics much since then.

I had a good relationship with Mike O'Callaghan,[2] but the press reported that Senator Cannon selected Mike to head the Clark County Democratic Central Committee so that in case I challenged Cannon for his seat in the Senate, Mike would be strategically placed to stop me. The press can be extremely imaginative; apparently, any straw in the wind would give fuel to that running-for-the-Senate fire. After you see so many of those things you just file them in the political wastebasket and forget them. In fact, Mike O'Callaghan became part of my administration, so at that point maybe he became a Sawyer man. He ran the Nevada Department of Human Resources, and he ran it very well.

Mike's a guy who works night and day. People tell the story that when he was governor he would be calling people at six o'clock in the morning and that sort of thing, which I must say I never did. (He had served in the military, as I had, but the effect of that service was a little different on him. [laughter]) Mike was a fine governor who was able to instill total loyalty in the people who work for him, and I have always been greatly impressed by that — people who admired him, admired him fully, and they still do. And he never got himself involved in any of the hanky-panky surrounding gaming licenses and that sort of thing that some other governors have been accused of. He appointed people who were capable; then he left them alone. His theory was the same as mine: if he didn't think they were doing a good job, he would get rid of them and get somebody else, but he wasn't going to sit down and negotiate on licenses and other actions that were properly within the purview of the Gaming Board or Gaming Commission.

Mike's eight years as governor were about as impressive as any in the history of Nevada. He is still very popular and very powerful, and anybody who runs for major public office these days who doesn't go by to see Mike O'Callaghan doesn't know what the hell he's doing. As executive editor of the *Las Vegas Sun* he's developed a totally non-partisan stance. He doesn't run that paper as a Democratic organ any more than the Greenspuns ran it as a Republican paper, nor does he endorse candidates much anymore . . . whereas I do. But I'm in a different situation. Mike has to appear to be impartial if his newspaper is to retain any credibility, and he has done that very effectively.

Mike is a bit more conservative than I am on some issues — because our backgrounds are somewhat different, we may be driven by different instincts. By and large, though, he is progressive and was a progressive governor, and, generally speaking, we're on the same side. We don't always back the same candidates, but we both understand that. Mike's a lot of fun to be around, and he has an excellent memory; much better than mine. [laughter]

The most disturbing political development in recent Nevada history occurred in 1982: Congressman James Santini entered the Democratic primary for U.S. senator against Howard Cannon, who had represented Nevada for eighteen years. I had known Jim Santini a long time — really knew him better than I knew Howard Cannon — and I had supported him vigorously in his various campaigns.[3] But when Jim came to me (and he went to a lot of other people as well) and said that he was thinking of running against Howard Cannon, I attempted to dissuade him. He would be running against an incumbent who had been doing a good job and had a fine record in the Senate, one who had accomplished a great deal for Nevada in many areas. I didn't want to see one popular Democratic office holder attempt to bootstrap himself up against a competent, distinguished senator of the same party, and I advised Jim that I thought it was a big mistake. I told him that I would support Senator Cannon, which I did, and I was quite confident that Cannon would defeat him.

Santini had been part of Nevada's congressional team for several years — working in concert with Cannon, as far as I knew — and to have him suddenly decide to feed his own ego by challenging an incumbent, simply because he wanted a higher position, violated all of the unwritten rules. He lost most of my respect by that move. In the rather nasty campaign that Santini mounted, he damaged not only Senator Cannon and himself, he did tremendous harm to the Democratic party; and, in my opinion, he hurt the state of Nevada, as well.

(I had had similar feelings about Teddy Kennedy's challenge of the incumbent Jimmy Carter for the presidential nomination in 1980, a challenge based less on substance than on the power of the Kennedy aura that he had inherited from his brother, John. Of course, there was a big difference between Teddy and Jim Santini: I had known Teddy for years, and seen him in action, and I doubted his judgment and maturity . . . and there were questions about his personal life. Not that I cared, except that he did not have enough sense to keep it private, as it should have been.)

Cannon narrowly won in the primary over Santini, but in the general election he lost to Republican Chic Hecht. I was shocked. Looking back on it, you have to credit Jim Santini with Hecht's victory — he had damaged Senator Cannon so badly in the primary. Going in to the election Hecht was totally unknown outside a relatively small circle of acquaintances in Las Vegas, while Senator Cannon was a powerful, distinguished presence in the United States Senate who had done much for Nevada. How could he lose? One of the things Cannon had done for his constituents was get the railroad out of downtown Elko. Elko had wanted this for years, but nobody could ever accomplish anything until Howard Cannon made it happen. But I'll be damned if Elko County — which wouldn't have known Chic Hecht from a bale of hay — didn't go for Hecht! It was crazy!

I was very active for Cannon, campaigning around the state for him. About two weeks before the election it was clear that there was something going on that we didn't understand, when a poll came out that had the candidates virtually even. I later heard that Cannon's advisors gave so little credence to the poll that they didn't think it worth discussing with the senator. By then it was probably too late to do anything, anyway — there had been some late-breaking publicity which was immediately seized upon by those who didn't want to support him. It was something to do with FBI wire taps, and . . . although the senator was called as a witness in an organized crime trial, he was never indicted for anything. Nothing was ever proven: he was never a target; he was never tried; but all those people who had doubts were given a reason to abandon him.

Hecht's victory was one of those upsets that defy explanation. Chic Hecht could have walked down the street anywhere in northern Nevada, and in many communities in southern Nevada, and *nobody* would have known who he was. Later, you would ask someone, "Well, why did you vote for Hecht?" Many voted for him just because he was a Republican; other explanations made even less sense. In the north there was still that anti-Clark County feeling that you always have to consider in a campaign: if you are thought to be a city slicker from Las Vegas, and Cannon was, they probably aren't going to vote for you. So that helped Hecht, whose victory was really a sad day for Nevada.

Had Howard Cannon been reelected we would not be fighting the nuclear dump battle here today, because his seniority and power could not have been taken lightly. Hecht was a freshman senator without seniority or respect, and there was another factor — he presumptively agreed that Nevada should be one of the sites for a nuclear dump. He went before our state legislature along with Senator Laxalt and gave a big speech about the duty of Nevadans to support national military objectives . . . apparently not knowing that this dump had nothing at all to do with military or defense capabilities! He didn't even know that it was a private consortium of utility companies trying to get rid of their waste! So we had both Republican senators supporting the location of a nuclear waste dump in Nevada. Howard Cannon, I am confident, would have fought vigorously to keep us off the list, and he had enough trading power with his seniority on various committees, appropriations and otherwise, to have succeeded. But in the 1980s we had Ronald Reagan in the White House, Paul Laxalt and Chic Hecht in the Senate, and Barbara Vucanovich in Congress . . . all Republicans.

In 1988, when Democratic Governor Richard Bryan successfully challenged Chic Hecht for his Senate seat, the nuclear waste dump was a major campaign issue, with Bryan adamantly opposed. In a memorable slip of the tongue Hecht referred to the proposed dump as a "nuclear suppository." [laughter] It was a classic gaffe that was reported all over the country. Bryan was very popular, and he jumped out to a lead in the polls that was simply incredible, but the contest turned into a horse race before it was over. By election day Bryan's lead was down to only four points. Credit for the turnaround has to go to Senator Hecht and his handlers: he was a pretty able tactician . . . either that, or he had people around him who did a hatchet job on Bryan. [laughter] It was unbelievable! Hecht took absolutely "nothing" items and succeeded in making them into overriding issues. In one case his people portrayed a state airplane as being effectively Bryan's personal plane, purchased with state money, and with the cooperation of the press they inflated this absurdity into a full-blown scandal. Bryan's people should have snuffed that fire out immediately, but they fiddled while Rome was burning. Bryan didn't understand what was happening until the last few weeks, when he moved to meet the issue. I even went on radio for him, but it was almost too late — the election appeared to be slipping away.[4]

Although Hecht lost, he later told me that he got more votes on that one charge than on any other issue in his whole campaign, and that shows you what can happen when you ignore things that you know are absurd, but the guy on the street doesn't. If a voter thinks you are taking tax money out of his pocket to ride around in a nice airplane which you have purchased for yourself, he's going to be incensed.

Dick Bryan and I have been political allies for a long, long time, and I know him to be a tireless worker who lives and breathes his job. He works long, hard hours, and he chooses to live close to the Senate Office Building so that he has ready access to his office. But he possesses other qualities that are even more impressive: he's an absolutely straight shooter who never lies, and he's a man of total integrity. If he says he's going to do something, he does it — you can put it in the bank — and he wouldn't accept a questionable dime even if he were penniless. Bryan is also fearless and consistent. He doesn't shift around. He doesn't start on something, then say, "Well, wait a minute here. This doesn't look too good for me; I'm going to change my position."

Dick's character is revealed in his sponsorship of a bill that assures that within the next few years gas-guzzling automobiles will be gone.[5] Now, that bill hasn't made a big impression in Nevada, but it made a *terrific* impression in Congress, where the automobile industry fought him tooth and nail. There was no reason that he had to take on this issue — it isn't anything particularly appealing or of interest to Nevadans — but Dick is convinced that if we are going to do something about the environment, we have to stop wasting money, time, and energy on gas guzzlers. It's this kind of thinking that I admire him for. He doesn't have to do this to be reelected in Nevada, and the forces arrayed against him . . . . Bennett Johnson, chairman of the energy committee and godfather of the effort to place the nuclear repository in Nevada, is from Louisiana, an oil and gas-producing state. Johnson keeps hinting that if Bryan would just come around on the automobile issue, he might not be so aggressive in trying to place the nuclear dump in Nevada. Isn't that a lot of bull? When the oil-producing people in the Senate line up against our junior senator from Nevada, it requires courage to take the heat. Richard Bryan takes it and he never backs off, and he's eventually going to get a bill through. He will be a great United States senator, and I thought he was a great governor.

Senator Harry Reid and Dick Bryan have very different personalities. Harry's a quiet, self-effacing man, and he is not a very good speaker — he's not particularly good in public, as compared with Dick Bryan. But it would be a big mistake to underestimate Harry Reid. His accomplishments in the Senate have been impressive, particularly his contributions to resolving the northern Nevada water dispute. Politicians as far back as Pat McCarran had attempted to do something about that and failed, and many of them were more powerful and had more leverage than Harry Reid has acquired in the short time he's been in the Senate. Harry was just doggedly persistent — he never quit; just kept toughing it out. And it must be recognized that it took statesmanship on his part to get his bill passed. There were a lot of potential political liabilities for him, and he took a lot of flak, yet he accomplished something which none of his predecessors had been able to do. There may be some things wrong with the resulting legislation, but already it has been shown to be generally quite beneficial.[6]

In his bill Senator Reid tried to balance conflicting interests in northern Nevada — Indians, agriculture, urban growth, and so on — and some powerful people are bitter about the legislation, because there's so little water to go around that they don't want to share it. I chalk the bill up as one of the most courageous and effective acts of federal legislation for Nevada that I've seen in a long time, and Harry accomplished it with relatively little fanfare, as he does most things.

Another way in which Harry may be a little different from Dick Bryan is in his intuitive understanding of how the political game is played. To become powerful you have to be able to play that game, and I think he is moving progressively into a position where he will be able to play it with great benefit to the state of Nevada. In politics, you and your colleagues must work together on issues; you must give and take; you have to be able to understand the conflicting interests in the Senate and know who the players are. I'm not saying that Dick Bryan doesn't, but I think that Harry Reid is probably more interested in the internal workings of the United States Senate, its committees and other things.

Politically adroit though he is, Senator Reid would never compromise his principles. We know how the citizens of Nevada feel about abortion — the vote was decisive in that area — and yet Harry has not changed his position. He remains steadfastly opposed to legalized abortion, even though that stance may have cost him a lot of votes when he stood for reelection.

As he gets more seniority and moves into better positions on committees, Harry Reid will be an outstanding senator, and it would be a shame if the people of Nevada didn't keep him in Washington. With a small state like ours, we have to have people with seniority in the Senate, because we'll never have much influence in the House of Representatives. Some of the biggest dunces ever born in America have wielded great power just because they acquired enough seniority to become chairmen of senate committees. That isn't always in the best interests of the American public, but that's the way government works, and Harry knows that. He and Dick Bryan ultimately will be in position to be very effective if we just have the good judgment to leave them in the Senate for a while.

This state has produced some powerful senators — William Stewart, Key Pittman, Pat McCarran, Alan Bible, Howard Cannon and others — and seniority was the source of their strength. Now, occasionally Nevada elects someone who is disinterested — that's unusual, but sometimes it happens — and you had better get rid of that person, because seniority won't make any difference if he's not going to do anything for his home state. Paul Laxalt sat on no important committees and passed no important legislation that affected the state of Nevada. But his type has been rare for this state over the years.

Congresswoman Barbara Vucanovich and I come down on opposite sides of most issues. She's very acute and politically sensitive, but she started out on the wrong foot on the nuclear repository issue, partially due, I'm sure, to the collegiality among herself, Paul Laxalt, Chic Hecht, and Ronald Reagan. But before any of the rest of them saw the light, Barbara did, and one day she woke up and said, "I'm on the wrong side of this issue." She didn't try to kid anybody about it; she didn't try to gild the lily. She simply said, "I am now against the nuclear dump. That's the way my constituents feel, and I represent my constituents." She switched, and she's been absolutely unswerving in her opposition to the repository since that great day.

Barbara, who was an aide to Senator Laxalt at one point, is extremely popular, and she has a very loyal ranching, mining, and agriculture constituency which I think she effectively represents. She's responsive to their needs, she answers all their letters, and she does the little things that keep people happy. She's gradually gaining seniority, but there are so many members in the House that it takes many years and numerous reelections to move into a position of power . . . which Barbara may yet attain. As respected and popular as Barbara is, nobody's going to touch her as long as she wants to run. In her district, I don't think you could beat her with a second coming. [laughter]

Jim Bilbray was in the state senate for a number of terms, and I wasn't terribly impressed with his performance. But, somewhat to my surprise, he has done an absolutely spectacular job in Congress. He has not made any major gaffes, and he has been innovative and imaginative and has handled himself like a pro. Jim certainly isn't a flaming liberal, but neither is his southern Nevada constituency. He calls things as he sees them, and he doesn't necessarily follow the party line on everything. As a consequence, I think he has a solid voting record.

Like Barbara Vucanovich, Bob List, Nevada's governor from 1979 through 1982, was always on the other side politically, and as a rule you don't get too buddy-buddy with people who don't share your interests or concerns. But I see Bob often now that he is in the same category that I am, ex-governor, and you forget about the political differences, whatever they might have been. He's a very amiable fellow, a nice guy, and I enjoy him. I think we've developed a mutual respect since he's been out of office.

So far as I can recall, there were no successful initiatives while he was governor. The ones that he did take — the tax shift, for example — didn't turn out too well politically. And he was hurt by the thing about accepting comps.[7] I don't pay any attention to those things, but if you're going to take comps, which everybody does at one time or another, you should use some judgment as to when and where and in whose company. Something like that shouldn't divert attention from the job you are doing as governor, but you can't separate the two in the public mind, and some of these silly little things get blown out of proportion.

Bob Miller's father ran the Riviera Hotel, and the first time I ran for governor he was one of my early supporters; those were few and far between on the Strip. [laughter] I got to know Bob's parents reasonably well, and I always liked and admired them. There may have been some reputed unsavory things in the father's past, but I didn't know about that; and I was interested in the guy I knew — not what some paper said had happened in Detroit thirty years ago.

When Bob came along I supported him just because he was a Democrat, but since he became acting governor and then governor I've gained great respect for him. He's a man of total integrity who wouldn't shade anything of substance or importance. Like Dick Bryan, if Bob Miller says in private, "This is the way I feel about an issue," that's the position you're going to see reported in the papers after he gives a public speech. He has been very forthright in his addresses to the legislature, and he really hasn't shifted from his policy positions even though he's had some very tough political decisions to make. We all know that any governor who's in office when taxes are increased very likely will be beaten the next election, whether he was responsible or not. But Bob had a decision to make that was fundamental to the operation of the state of Nevada, and he did the right thing.

Everybody says, "Gee, we're the fastest-growing state in America!" That's terrific, but people have to understand that with growth comes a need for additional revenues; there's no way around it. And we have run out of revenue in Nevada. If we are to continue operating without violating the state constitution by deficit spending, we simply have to increase revenues. Gaming has a very strong lobby, of course, and in Governor Miller's first budget crisis they took the position that if their taxes were increased they would go broke. (I wonder if that was really the case.) But revenues had to be raised, and Bob Miller did as well as anyone could in a no-win situation such as that. Now, the legislation that was eventually passed by the legislature was theirs, not his, but when you're governor you're held responsible for drought, floods, a weak economy, and everything else. [laughter] So I'm afraid that in the public mind much of the onus for that tax increase fell on him. Bob Miller came along at a time when, for the good of Nevada, the issue of higher taxes had to be faced, and he faced it.

14

statesmen and other political creatures

My mother was very fond of FDR, and, therefore, when I was growing up I was too; but I couldn't say why, other than that he was a Democrat and he appeared to be a social liberal, as my mother was. In truth, as a young man I had no well-defined philosophy of government that went beyond my instincts, and FDR died before I had matured to the point where I began to hold some of the ideas that I have today. The day that the United States declared war against Japan, I went with McCarran to the House of Representatives to hear the president's speech, and I was shocked to see that FDR couldn't walk. I didn't know he had been unable to walk all the time that he was president. Even to stand up, he had to be helped, and I saw that his braces were fixed so he could stand while delivering the request for a declaration of war. Of course, in those days there was far less publicity and less glare on major public figures than there is now. Surely today if a crippled person ran for office, every voter would know.

So far as national politics were concerned, I wasn't paying attention through much of the 1940s — being in the army was like living in another world, and while I was in law school, studies absorbed all of my time and energy. It wasn't until I was admitted to the bar and went to Elko that I entered the dialogue, and then the "communist threat" that was so much discussed didn't worry me. Even in those days I was more concerned about the real enemy within — police state tactics, the power of the FBI, the American people being disenfranchised by their own government — than I was about communists. Senator Joe McCarthy's witch hunts, and J. Edgar Hoover, and the secret government that was controlling our lives were what truly troubled me.

By background and inclination an avid Democrat, I had little tolerance for Republicans as a rule — I was for the Democrats, whoever they were and whatever office they were seeking . . . but I didn't appreciate Harry Truman then as I do now. (I think that's true of most of us.) He came out of what appeared to be a rather tawdry political background, and out of a political machine where most people were tainted;[1] but he came out with a refreshing candor, unapologetic about the whole thing.

Truman was different. He looked like a shoe clerk who had gotten lucky, and he never stooped to any of the cheap political tendencies of many of our recent presidents. In fact, he was so real that it almost seemed like a facade — nobody could be that real, so he had to be play-acting in some way, and you suspected that the things that he was doing were just for show or for some sort of political advantage. But it turned out that Truman was just that kind of guy, and he had not been particularly affected by the phoniness of politics.

While I was governor I tried to get Harry Truman to speak in Nevada, initially without success. Finally, in 1960, he accepted my invitation. Bette and I met him at the airport, and we rode in an open car to the University of Nevada campus, which was the only place where he would agree to speak . . . and he would not stay overnight, either. [laughter] In those days national political figures were just scared to death of Nevada. (Eleanor Roosevelt once had her picture taken next to a slot machine, and it caused a sensation throughout the country.) Most national politicians who would come here at all were either making a campaign whistle-stop, or were here for some specific purpose and would not stay overnight because they didn't want to be in the vicinity of gaming casinos. Not even Harry Truman would sleep over.

As we were going down the street heading for the campus, Bette said, "Mr. President, I just dread these parades. You ride along and people boo you, give you the finger; I just dread them."

Truman said, "Well, young lady, I'll tell you, nobody has ever been booed in the history of politics as much as I have. And what I do is just smile and wave; and if I can get close enough, I kick them in the ass!" [laughter]

Truman was an unusual man who *did* get lucky, but America got lucky, too, when he came along. He was totally different from Roosevelt in every way, and having been a Roosevelt admirer I wondered how this farmer-type guy ever got to be president of the United States. None of the glamour, none of the pizzazz that you had been used to with Roosevelt; none of the class or sophistication. But that time in American politics was made for a Harry Truman, and history would confirm his greatness.

Adlai Stevenson was just fantastic. He was an erudite intellectual, sophisticated and articulate, and he used the English language like a musical instrument. Stevenson wasn't the kind of person that you would usually see in politics. He almost came out of another world, and here was this marvelous, intellectual person running for president. I had nothing in particular against Dwight Eisenhower, but he came off pretty much as a peasant compared to Adlai Stevenson and in the 1950s I was more into party loyalty and contempt for all Republicans than I am today, or have been for several years. Looking back, I now think that Eisenhower was a lot smarter than I believed at the time; in fact, he was a good president.

About Richard Nixon I have very different feelings: his campaigns in California horrified me . . . Jerry Voorhis; then Helen Gahagan Douglas . . . . [2] I thought Nixon was a charlatan of the first order, and I was constantly amazed that he had gotten to where he was. I always felt that if there was any kind of just retribution in this life, at some point they had to uncover this fake; and eventually, of course, that's what happened. I had no sympathy for Richard Nixon, either before or after he became president of the United States. Everything he did revolted me.

In 1958, during my campaign for governor, John Kennedy came to town and campaigned for me, and we started a strong and lasting friendship. I was enchanted. He was everything that any young political figure aspires to be — sophisticated, bright, very witty, good looking — and his personal magnetism was as strong in private as it was in public. He had that great ability to put everybody at ease, and he had not the slightest pretense . . . at least, none that you could see. [laughter] Folks were struck by Kennedy. They said, "Gee, I wish I was that good looking; that I had the kind of background he has; that I was as clever as he is," but I didn't suspect then that he would be the political idol that he later became.

Richard M. Nixon clasps Gov. Sawyer's hand during a Nevada stop in his
1959 campaign again John F. Kennedy. *"I thought Nixon was a charlatan
of the first order . . . . "*

Gov. Sawyer meets with President John F. Kennedy in the Oval Office, 1961. *"Many of our meetings were not publicized. You didn't tell the public that you were having a private meeting with the president of the United States unless he wanted it announced."*

In 1960 I arranged for Kennedy to address a joint session of the state legislature, which wasn't necessarily a big deal — you would do this for any serious candidate for president who was campaigning in Nevada. In conjunction with that event Bette and I decided to have a reception for him at the mansion (we had furniture by then!), and we sent out invitations to people all over the state. When Kennedy and Pierre Salinger and their party got to Reno, they eluded the press and sneaked off in a car and went up to Lake Tahoe and looked it over before coming to Carson City. We weren't sure exactly when to expect them, but they arrived at the governor's mansion a couple of hours before the reception was slated to begin. Bette met them at the door — John Kennedy with a suit cover over his arm, and Pierre Salinger — and they made some apologies for arriving early. Bette had curlers in her hair, and she was terribly embarrassed and completely surprised, but they came in and made themselves at home. We had a nice piano downstairs in the mansion, and Salinger (who had been some sort of child prodigy on the piano) sat down and started to play. I was taking a shower when Bette came upstairs and said, "Senator Kennedy is here."

I said, "Well, tell him to come in."

He came in and sat on the toilet while I finished my shower, and we talked a little. Then he changed his clothes and I got ready for the reception.

We had a drink or two, and it was time to form the reception line. By then there were literally hundreds of people from throughout the state lined up in front of the mansion waiting to get in, and it was quite a cool evening, so we wanted to get everybody inside. We started quickly feeding these people through. We had put out punch and cookies for them, and all went smoothly, and for two or three hours people came through shaking hands and so on. It was a whiz-bang affair, a lot of fun, and Senator Kennedy thoroughly enjoyed it; he was very gregarious. It was the first time I think something like that had been done with a presidential candidate before he had won any primaries.

At the national convention in 1960 the choices boiled down to Kennedy, Lyndon Johnson, and Adlai Stevenson. I was always very fond of Adlai, admired his presence and his intellect, respected what he stood for, but I had come to the conclusion that he wasn't electable; and I just personally didn't care for Lyndon Johnson, to be perfectly frank. But Jack Kennedy was a breath of fresh air. I thought he would be able to move in directions that I approved of, faster and more effectively than anyone else. There was never any doubt in my mind, but I did not state publicly that I would support him — I didn't want to get out front too early and have delegates begin to focus on me as a reason for their opposition to Kennedy; he was the candidate, not me, and I didn't want him to pick up enemies that I might have out there.

The stories of Kennedy's victory and subsequent brief presidency are well known. It was, as the press put it, Camelot revisited; not only did I feel that way, but obviously a lot of other people did, too. The country was ready for a change, and he was ready to lead it, and I wanted to do everything I could to help him. Nevada was the only state in the Far West that he carried, and I was the only major political figure in Nevada who supported him — I campaigned hard for him.

Although President Kennedy gave the impression that he was above petty political maneuvering, obviously he wasn't . . . and his brother Bobby *certainly* wasn't. [laughter] But Jack gave the impression that he was on a little higher plane, and that he wasn't interested in the seamier things that political people had to do. He never criticized anybody to me; he never even talked to me about the personal foibles of others. Politicians usually sit down and exchange stories about one another, but I never got any of that from him.

Virtually every time I went to Washington I would see President Kennedy, but many of our meetings were not publicized. You didn't tell the public that you were having a private meeting with the president of the United States unless he wanted it announced, and after a meeting it was entirely up to him to reveal its subject, if he wanted to. To be perfectly candid about it, I occasionally made up some more-or-less superficial reason, such as the Battle Mountain flood, for our meetings. The president was not going to spend an awful lot of time worrying about the Battle Mountain flood, but it did me some good if people in Battle Mountain thought I was talking to the president about their flood — and I did mention it to him. Of course, you are both in the same business, and if your relationship is strong the president might say, "You can use this meeting for whatever good it can do you, governor." He might also say, "Look, when we're through here if you want to make an announcement, fine. This is roughly what you should say." But I always felt that it was solely the executive's prerogative to make any public statements about a private meeting, and I never quoted him on any meeting I ever had with him. If a president can't meet privately with you without fear of some errant statement to the press later, he's not going to meet with you anymore.

The political impact of President Kennedy's assassination is very hard to assess because he wasn't in office long enough for one to judge whether or not he would have been an effective president; and most of his initiatives were concluded under President Johnson . . . possibly more successfully and faster than they would have been under President Kennedy. Who knows? And some seamy things of a personal nature have come out since which might have taken the luster off his presidency had they been disclosed while he was alive. But

in the short time that he was president, John Kennedy set a
whole new direction and established a new perspective for
America. Even had he been unable to do more than enunciate
the things that he wanted for this country, that still meant a
great deal. John Kennedy came at the right time for America.
The country was tired, cynical, and disillusioned at that point,
and he set some lofty goals and ideals and began to reener-
gize the public. He lifted the spirits of the American people
to a greater extent than anyone has during my lifetime, even
though his actual legislative accomplishments weren't that
impressive.

Kennedy never discussed Vietnam with me, but according
to historical accounts that I have read, he further entrenched
us there. (Perhaps his ultimate decision would have been to
get us out as quickly as possible. I do know that Vietnam
turned out to be absolute political death for Lyndon Johnson.)
The Cuban missile crisis falls into the same category: if you
were for President Kennedy and you were enchanted by him,
as I was, you were just thrilled by the way he handled it. On
the other hand, anti-Kennedy people came up with a lot of
things they thought he should have done differently. I don't
know, except that he was successful: the missiles were
removed, we stayed at peace, and the spirits of all Americans
were raised. This was sort of a David and Goliath thing — we
had been hearing about all the Russian power, and here was
this young guy standing up and saying, "Don't go another
foot!" He got away with it, and Americans were really thrilled
by that. He was one of my heroes. Right through to his death
I remained as close to him as our situations would permit,
and I will say for him that John Kennedy was a person who
remembered his friends.

I was so fond of Eleanor Roosevelt that a couple of years after I became governor I wrote and asked if I could come see her. (That's when she was living in New York and was our representative to the United Nations.) She wrote back a very chatty note saying, "Well, of course, come up and see me." A date was set, and when I was in New York on other business I went to her apartment. She lived on the third floor of a brownstone with no elevator, and I walked up three flights to her apartment, and there was a German lady there. Eleanor had still not come home from the United Nations that day, so the lady seated me and I waited.

About half an hour later I heard footsteps climbing the stairs, and in came Eleanor Roosevelt, international celebrity, with an armload of groceries which she had stopped and bought for the house — just as common and ordinary as anybody could possibly be! It was just like visiting your grandmother: "How are you doing? Have a seat. Can I get you some coffee?" and so on. We sat there and talked for a couple of hours, and she didn't want to talk about herself at all, and she didn't want to talk about FDR . . . she wanted to know about me. It's always gratifying when somebody else shows an interest in you. "Tell me about Nevada. What's it like there? Tell me about the people. How did you get started in politics?" Now, I was a total throwaway as far as Eleanor Roosevelt was concerned, I'm sure; but she was the most engaging, warmest, most interesting person I've ever talked to, and I was captivated by her. You felt she wanted to take the whole world in her arms and help everybody. It was a wonderful afternoon.

The first time I met Lyndon Johnson was shortly after I was elected, and he was Senate majority leader. I went to Washington, and Alan Bible took me by to see "the leader." It was somewhat difficult to understand this great reverence for him, but this was how it worked: the leader was the leader; you didn't call him by his name, you called him "the leader," and there was no question that he was feared and revered among United States senators. Bible took me in and introduced me to Lyndon, who told me what a great fellow I was. He had *no idea* who he was talking to, but he said I was the savior of the state of Nevada and all these great things. Then he reached into the bottom drawer of his desk and came up with a pair of cuff links . . . I guess majority leader cuff links or something. He indicated that I was one of the few people he had ever bestowed this great honor on. [laughter] It was a performance that left me feeling a little unclean. Later he asked me to help him with his last presidential campaign, and I actually found that I had some sympathy for him. But up to that point I had always felt almost as if I should wash my hands after every meeting with Lyndon Johnson.

After Jack Kennedy was assassinated I met with President Johnson; this was in early December, 1963. I complained bitterly about Robert Kennedy and J. Edgar Hoover, as I was wont to do in those days to anybody who would listen to me; and in reply the president had few, if any, positive things to say about Bobby Kennedy, who had excluded him from the whole governmental process all the time that Jack was president. Lyndon Johnson had been humiliated. As a matter of fact, Johnson told me in his own earthy language that when John Kennedy died, Bobby had the Oval Office sealed so that he could not get into the president's office! Johnson literally had to force his way into the Oval Office to assume

Grant Sawyer is greeted by President Lyndon B. Johnson, 1965. *"I always felt almost as if I should wash my hands after every meeting with Lyndon Johnson."*

his duties as president, and he was very descriptive about what he thought of Bobby. [laughter] But there wasn't much he could do about it.

Everyone feared Johnson. He was a vindictive guy, and his whole history had shown that if you got on the wrong side of him, you had better be careful. This made his antipathy toward Hoover ironic — here you had two people of about the same caliber, operating primarily on the basis of fear . . . . In those days *many* in Washington feared Hoover, including his immediate boss, Attorney General Bobby Kennedy.

J. Edgar Hoover was an American folk hero whose ego was as big as Bobby Kennedy's, and there was an intense rivalry between the two. Hoover stood in Bobby's way. Bobby would have loved to have gotten rid of him, but there was that blackmail situation; he had to be careful: "I certainly wouldn't want anybody to know about it, but I've learned this and that about you. I will do everything in my power to protect you." That was Hoover's line.

People were literally in a panic because of all the private dossiers that Hoover had compiled . . . and that included files on presidents of the United States, Lyndon Johnson among them. People in government didn't know whether Bobby had access to those dossiers or not, but there was widespread reluctance to take any action against either Hoover or Bobby for fear that you would end up the victim; and although Johnson may have been immodest and unrestrained, he understood his own background and the facts of life in Washington, and he was not about to put himself in a position where someone could harpoon him publicly with some dossiers.

Johnson and I got along OK after a while, but I don't know why . . . as a matter of fact I'm not sure that I ever did learn to understand and appreciate him. I am no goody two shoes, but he had some personal habits that were repulsive to me — he was very crude, and I always had the feeling, even after I got to know him reasonably well, that some way or other I was being conned. When Johnson ran for the presidential nomination against Jack Kennedy, Bob Strauss and John Connally of Texas came to Nevada to meet with me about his candidacy. They were vying for the Nevada delegation — the contest was that close in their minds. They asked what I wanted in return for delivering Nevada, and offers of Secretary of the Interior and other things were held out: "Whatever you want, you can have." Well, I happened to know that they were doing the same thing in other states with some of my governor colleagues, so I wasn't terribly impressed with any of that. It was all just the sort of con that was coming out of that camp, and I thought it was rather typical of Lyndon Johnson.

In departure from what a lot of Washington insiders thought of Nevada, however, President Johnson really had a good impression of this state. He appeared at a Democratic state convention in Ely and made the major speech, and he was in and out of Nevada a lot due to his respect for Senator Bible, to whom he was very responsive. Lyndon was quite an earthy guy, as everybody knows, and he didn't pass moral judgment on the gambling and prostitution in Nevada — during his presidency we didn't have any sense of being looked down upon and discriminated against. I think he liked the people of Nevada, and certainly the people of Nevada supported him at the polls.

John Kennedy was assassinated before he had an opportunity to do something about most of his goals, but Lyndon Johnson, who was much more influential with Congress, moved forcefully and effectively to implement them. (Kennedy was always kind of an outsider to the Congress.) Johnson probably got more substantive legislation passed in a shorter period of time than any president in history, with the possible exception of Franklin Roosevelt. So he was certainly a leader in that sense.

In 1964 my name was tossed around as a possible vice-presidential running mate for Johnson, and the Nevada delegation passed a resolution supporting my candidacy . . . once in a while you run into one of those old Johnson/Sawyer buttons at a swap meet or something. This sort of talk usually starts when a presidential candidate needs support: you make hints to governors in the expectation that they will then get out and really hump for you, so you have a whole bunch of aspiring vice-presidential-candidate governors trying to lead their delegations to support your nomination. That has never changed; it's still the same. But I didn't take these things seriously. Pat McCarran had told me years before that nobody from Nevada was ever going to be a president or vice-president of the United States, and probably none would hold a cabinet position, because of the generally-held perception of Nevada. I agreed with that assessment. In 1964 I knew that the vice presidency was not going to happen — it was just that simple.

My personal feelings about LBJ notwithstanding, I came out early in support of his Vietnam policy, about which I didn't have misgivings at the time. I felt we were going to win the war, and I certainly felt that we *should* win it . . . do whatever we needed to do. A couple of years later I reassessed the situation and revised my view of the war, and when I now read some of the speeches I gave during that period I wince at my perception of it. By the time of the 1968 Democratic National Convention in Chicago, to which I was a delegate, I was opposed to the war. Many of the violent things that went on outside the hall, things that I later saw on television and read about in the newspapers, I was unaware of at the time they were happening . . . inside, we missed a lot of that, even though we knew it was a turbulent, chaotic situation that represented a watershed in the history of the Democratic party. Despair and hopelessness were gradually setting in throughout the country over the war in Vietnam. We were losing our own people and killing countless thousands of others with no purpose; and we weren't going to win . . . it wasn't a war that our policy *committed* us to win. The whole thing was just useless and damaging, and I had come full circle in just two years. At the convention I delivered the minority report of the resolutions committee — the peace plank.

Following the rules changes of 1968, the first Democratic nominee was George McGovern, whom I knew only slightly. In 1972 McGovern and his people pushed through some reforms that brought quotas into play in the national Democratic party. It became a numbers game. Your delegation to the Democratic National Convention had to include an Indian; it had to be 50 percent women; some percentage had to be old; some had to be young; so many had to be minorities . . . . This completely upset the whole system of selecting presidents and determining party affairs: the "good old boys" who had always met in smoke-filled rooms to decide these things suddenly were out. In George McGovern's Democratic party, even sitting governors and United States senators had to run against their own constituents for a chance to be a state delegate to the national convention and cast a vote for president!

We wound up with a polyglot of delegates, most of whom were not interested in anything beyond their own special interests. Before the reforms, most national committeemen were pros who had held public office or had been involved in party politics for years, had faced their constituents, and were relatively pragmatic about selecting someone who could win . . . and they were courted by all of the presidential candidates, because they were automatic delegates to the national convention. They, rather than a senator or governor, often led their state's delegation, and they were big players nationally. But as soon as the McGovern system was imposed, the whole idea of those guys sitting around deciding who was going to be president was no longer fair: "That's not democratic! Let Democrats who have little or no experience make the decisions, because they represent the people. You don't."

As soon as "the people" got in, they tossed out all the old guys: in reality, the reforms disenfranchised those Democrats who had faced the electorate and won, because by the time we got through filling all the quotas, there was no room for anyone who had proven himself or herself in the political arena, in judgment and ability. We went several years when none who had been major players could participate in Democratic party affairs, and holders of political office were practically excluded from an active role in the national convention! The only way they could attend as delegates was if they helped fill some kind of a minority quota.

I'm almost sorry to report this, because my position now is at variance with my general feelings about the way a democracy should work; as a matter of fact, it is contrary to the way I voted on the reforms in the national committee. I had accepted the idea that our party's whole approach was undemocratic — that a few people in the back room were making all the decisions — and I agreed that we should open the process up. We did; and soon every small special-interest group had a voice in national Democratic affairs. Now both the local and national Democratic party structures are virtually irrelevant, particularly when the incumbent president is not a

Democrat. The reason for having a party structure used to be to *elect* people . . . the decline in our effectiveness has been serious.

The McGovern reforms are with us today more in spirit than in fact, because party candidates are now selected in primaries before the national conventions. But their impact was powerful, and it lingers. In my opinion the '72 reforms and all of the succeeding quota and special-interest concessions by the Democratic party were fallout from the one-man, one-vote movement and the Supreme Court's 1964 reapportionment decision. In part because the Republican party wasn't as quick as the Democrats to let the so-called "people" in and keep the pros out, we had only one Democratic president in twenty-four years prior to Bill Clinton's election, and Jimmy Carter's victory was a fluke more attributable to the Watergate scandal than to competent planning.

In Nevada we went through the embarrassing process of having to elect Senator Howard Cannon to be a delegate to the national convention, and the election was *seriously* contested. Cannon had to run against one of his own constituents, and we went through several ballots before we finally elected him. That's a no-win situation for an office holder, so after the reforms most of them didn't even attend the conventions to which, in the old days, they would have been automatic delegates. The party became little more than a panoply of special-interest groups, none of whom gave a damn about anything but their own special interest. Even with Clinton's election, the Democratic party continues to flounder. We still have groups of people who are out only for their own interests; they could care less about the principal responsibility of a party in our democratic system, which is to elect people to office . . . namely, presidents. As long as they get their resolution passed or whatever, that's all they care about.

You say, "But look: this is going to hurt our chances to elect a president."

They say, "I don't give a damn about that; this is important to me."

The Republicans were much less eager about all this, and they didn't reform to anywhere near the extent that we Democrats did. That may be one reason that they did so well nationally for two decades — they were better at keeping control in the hands of knowledgeable people. The Democratic party, meanwhile, had nothing for middle America; middle America, therefore, kept demolishing Democratic candidates until George Bush blew his own chances for reelection.

I was very close to Governor Pat Brown of California, and although we seldom saw one another after we left office, we stayed in touch through mutual friends and so on. We were neighboring governors who ran at the same time; we were elected at the same time; and we communicated frequently during and after those campaigns. Pat came to my inauguration and I went to his; and where it would do him some good I would go into his state and make an appearance, and he would do the same thing for me in Nevada. So we felt sort of a western kinship.

I had the highest respect for Pat. We differed on some issues, like Lake Tahoe, and he may have acted a little foolish in public on occasion, but so did I. [laughter] The important thing was that he never said anything to me privately that he wasn't willing to say and take a stand on publicly — in fact, I was sometimes a little startled at what he would say to the press! [laughter] You never felt that Pat was doing something purely for political effect; quite the contrary, he sometimes took positions that he knew could be politically damaging, the Caryl Chessman case being an excellent example. Chessman was a convicted murderer who had been sentenced to die in the gas chamber, but Pat, as a matter of conscience, was opposed to capital punishment, and he wanted to commute Chessman's sentence. This unfolded in 1960 at about the time of the Winter Olympics at Lake Tahoe, where Pat and I were both in attendance as governors of neighboring states sharing the Games. Pat was introduced, and the whole stadium rocked with boos repudiating his wish to spare Chessman. But he had the courage not only to take the position, but to stay with it in the face of voter hostility. That takes guts! He was quite bright, a consummate political person, and a high-class fellow, and I thought Pat Brown was one of the best governors California ever had. I do not have the same enthusiasm for his son.

In 1976, Pat called to tell me that his son was going to run for president, and he would appreciate it if I could give him some help. I didn't know Jerry very well, so I asked Pat to have him come over to Las Vegas so we could get acquainted. Following our meeting I went back to my office and called Pat and said, "Pat, I love you like a brother but I don't think I can support your son."

He said, "Why?"

I said, "Well, you know, we talked for maybe an hour, and in that time he didn't say a single thing that made any sense to me." [laughter] Jerry had talked about how the first shall come last, and he was sleeping on the floor, and he would drive the old Chevy . . . and it just made no sense to me, whatsoever. I told Pat, "I'm concerned that he may not fully grasp the facts of life." Pat was not pleased, and I felt bad about it, but Nevada's votes weren't going to make or break Jerry, anyway. So I backed Jimmy Carter in 1976, co-chairing his campaign in Nevada with Jon Collins. But Bette said, "Look, we can't run out on Pat and Bernice — they are our friends." So she supported Jerry Brown, and she was the co-chairperson of his campaign in Nevada while I co-chaired Carter's.

After that Jerry went to the Democratic National Convention in New York City, where he roomed in a flea trap and boasted that he wasn't going to stay in any fancy hotel, and all of this stuff . . . which I thought was a cheap political stunt. He still hasn't said anything that makes any sense to me.

In 1976 I was still the national committeeman from Nevada when Jimmy Carter was nominated. I remember this little fellow coming in and walking around, shaking hands with everybody . . . nobody knew who he was. People would say, "Who's that guy?"

"Oh, he's running for president."

"Well, who is he? I can't remember his name." This happened over and over. I can't tell you the number of functions that I attended where this same little man was walking around shaking everybody's hand. About Carter, everybody will tell similar stories at national committee meetings where you are having private cocktail parties, and caucuses, or something. Nobody took him seriously, and I was not an early supporter of his; but when he became the nominee, my law partner, Jon Collins, and I became his state co-chairmen. I always supported the Democratic nominee for president.

After Carter was elected, I attended his inauguration. His wife, Rosalyn, was particularly impressive. She was really something! She was very bright, had steely determination, and was as active during his presidency as any president's wife ever was, with the possible exception of Eleanor Roosevelt . . . . Of course, you can't be sure that Eleanor and FDR communicated very much — she was doing her own thing most of the time. But Rosalyn was really a significant part of the Carter team, even in making policy. She was very well informed, and had all the right instincts; and, possibly, her judgment was a bit better than her husband's.

Carter's four-year presidency, I'm sorry to say, was an absolute disaster. Here was a bright, bright man, and he was certainly as well intentioned as anyone could have been. A man of great integrity, he just didn't have the capacity to run the executive branch of the United States government. He got *so* bogged down in details. We criticize Reagan for being completely neglectful — he simply turned over the government to his appointees and went to sleep — but Carter was just the opposite: he simply couldn't delegate and leave people alone and let them do their jobs. You had the feeling that he would add up the dinner tab to be sure it was right rather than just let some aide pay it. [laughter] And when he made a political move, it virtually always turned out to be the wrong one. He was a disaster.

Jimmy Carter didn't seem to comprehend how Congress operated or to understand the needs of congressmen, and the "good old boys" club on the hill looked on him as an outsider . . . which he was. He ran as an outsider against them, and they never forgave him, and he didn't have the inclination to bring them into his camp, as many presidents do and should. Congress always had the idea that they were going to show this cracker what the game is all about. They did a pretty good job. He was unable to cope with them.

Carter's foreign policy was strong on human rights, as, at the time, I thought it should be. Succeeding administrations often took the position that we were not going to get involved; that our aid wouldn't depend on what a country did to its own citizens in the area of equal rights. In the last ten or twelve years we haven't used our substantial monetary influence to try effect change, and I thought that was indefensible. However, as I see the big picture now, we can't reform the world; we can't insist that everyone embrace our form of democracy. I am not an isolationist (we still have to do business with other countries) but I no longer think it should be an all-or-nothing proposition, as it seemed to be with Carter. That's a delicate area of foreign policy that should be played pragmatically. We must recognize that other cultures are different from ours, and we should exert what pressure we can to effect democratic reforms without insisting that every country operate under our Bill of Rights. But Carter went overboard on demanding reform, just as Reagan ignored the problem totally. I agreed with neither of them. We can influence, but we ought not to demand.

Critical though I am of his administration, Jimmy Carter was, and is, a wonderful human being, and I believe some of his problems can be traced to bad luck. The perception of him now is a lot better than when he was president — he has turned out to be a great *ex*-president! But his wasn't the right personality at the right time to be president of the United States.

I didn't know Ronald Reagan when he was governor of California — Reagan was elected at the same time that Paul Laxalt succeeded me as governor in Nevada, and he wasn't a player while I was governor. Strictly from the perspective of an outside observer, though, I thought Reagan was a terrible governor and later a terrible president . . . and yet he's kind of like Frank Sinatra, who is still the biggest draw in town! This proves to me once again, if proof were needed, that my reactions are not always mainstream. [laughter]

I thought Reagan was a joke as president. He slept his way
through eight years . . . he appointed people to do his job,
and he thus felt freed from any responsibility. We hadn't
elected these guys, but they were totally running everything,
and there was no way we could get rid of them. But even
though Reagan was so hands-off that he really wasn't there,
he was probably the most popular president we've ever had.
(He's losing some of his lustre now, which I guess is what
normally happens when you become "ex" anything, except
for Jimmy Carter, who is looking better every day based on
what he's done since he was president.)

Reagan deserved his reputation as the great communicator,
although he never turned me on. He was everybody's Uncle
Ronny; they all loved him, and many people still do — he
still has that persona. Reagan had the great ability to say one
thing and do another without blinking an eyelash, just smiling
his way through . . . and it didn't seem to bother anybody!
The guy had some sort of magnetism that defied all logic, at
least in my book. But those who were around him are in
large part responsible for saddling this country with a debt
that will haunt us for generations to come.

You know, everybody does something sometime that you
agree with. My feeling about Reagan, however, was that no
matter what the policy, I couldn't be sure it was his, because
he was taking his naps every afternoon and swimming every
day. He had a leisurely eight years as president of the United
States without being affected by the problems and the duties
of the presidency. Others were handling that for him — he
just read the scripts, and he read them very well. Reagan was
an enigma to me, and I never understood how he could
remain so popular.

I supported Walter Mondale's campaign for the presidency, but many Democrats sat it out. It was a miserable campaign, second only to the later one of Dukakis in terms of sheer incompetence. Anybody that inept in a campaign couldn't be a very good president . . . . Mondale was a high-class, intelligent guy, and yet it was just one blunder after another. But maybe we have to give some credit to the Republicans for those seemingly awful Democratic gaffes — they have been much more clever at handling campaigns.

Geraldine Ferraro's presence on the ticket with Mondale was a political decision which probably hurt overall, but how can you say that the selection of a vice-president makes much difference? Look at Danny Quayle! [laughter] Now, if having him on the ticket were going to affect an election, Bush would have gone down to resounding defeat. Quayle was considered a joke when he was selected, and he has been ever since, yet that didn't seem to affect Bush's chances in the election.

15

---

who owns nevada ?

The Washington bureaucracy had such contempt for Nevada and her citizens! We endured their disdain when I was working in Senator McCarran's office, and in later years it only got worse. Washington still affects a certain snotty superiority, even today. There's something about Nevada: the whole composite of divorce, gambling, prostitution, and the years of dealing with the presence of the mob . . . . If you were from Nevada, you were thought to be not quite respectable, and the proposed Yucca Mountain nuclear dump is part of that legacy: "Nevada is a wasteland, and if we have some vile project that nobody else will tolerate, put it in Nevada!"

Congress passed legislation in 1972 to establish a site for the disposal of high-level nuclear waste — waste which is being produced, interestingly enough, not by the military or any other government agency, but by private nuclear power plants located around the country. Some of the plants have been in existence for close to forty years. They have accumulated a great deal of highly toxic, extremely dangerous material as a by-product from the operation of nuclear reactors, and they have nowhere safe to put it. So Congress decided that a site should be selected on federal land to be a deep, geological resting place for all of this radioactive waste.

At first there was relatively little concern in Nevada about the selection process, but as time went by and the range of possible locations began to narrow (mostly for political reasons) it became evident that we were the likely target. The state legislature created the Nevada Commission on Nuclear Projects to find ways to protect our interests.[1] Governor Richard Bryan appointed me to chair the commission, which included Michon Mackedon from Fallon and Ann Pierce from Reno; a labor representative and a Chamber of Commerce representative from Las Vegas; Ron Lurie from the League of Cities; and Thalia Dondero, representing the League of Counties. Ron Lurie was later replaced by Jan Laverly Jones, the mayor of Las Vegas.

We hardly knew what to do first, so we started by holding hearings to get the feel of what was going on. We invited Department of Energy (DOE) people and some state people to these hearings, and then we became interested in what role Congress was playing in all of this. So the whole commission traveled to Washington and interviewed various key players, including Bennett Johnson, the chairman of the senate energy committee. As time went by, and we learned more, it began to seem to some of us that the site selection process was being manipulated in Congress so that it would eventually, but inevitably, lead to Nevada through the back door. And indeed, that turned out to be true.

Initially nine possible locations for a repository had been identified, but as Republican senators in other states came up for election they would go to the president and say, "Look, you have to let me off the hook on this. I'm coming up for reelection; as long as my state is still on the list, I'm going to be defeated." So one by one, potential sites were eliminated for purely political reasons. Finally they got down to three, two of which, on the face of it, were just absurd. One was in Texas, but Vice-President Bush came from Texas, and the Speaker of the House was from Texas, and the proposed Texas site was over the largest underground aquifer in the United States, and . . . . [laughter] Another suggested site was in the state of Washington, where there was already a nuclear plant that had generated radioactive waste which was seeping into the Columbia River. That left Nevada. The whole thing was little more than a charade! Finally, Congress just dropped all pretense, and in 1987 said, "Yucca Mountain is going to be the site."

We have a very strange situation here: of the 116 private utilities around the country which have nuclear waste that they wish to get rid of, none are located in Nevada; and we finally discovered that the Yucca Mountain project being pushed by a federal agency is totally financed by those utilities to the tune of $600 million a year. The money goes to the Treasury, and Senator Bennett Johnson's energy committee then appropriates those funds to the Department of Energy for use at Yucca Mountain. In addition to the $600 million for the project, another $30 million that we know of is to be spent independently in Nevada to convince us of what a good deal it is! The Department of Energy is lending its scientists to the nuclear power industry to be trained by public relations people like Kent Oram. You see them on television every night telling us how safe their scheme is.

Nevada produces no nuclear waste of its own, yet the most expensive political campaign in the history of the state is going on now to assure us that radioactive waste is nice and safe, and that we should "relax and enjoy it." [laughter] But the bottom line is, if nuclear waste is all that safe, why don't the states where it comes from keep it? We are talking about a ten-thousand year situation here, longer than the history of civilization! I have asked them, "Well, tell me, what was Yucca Mountain like ten thousand years ago? How can you assure us that it will be safe for ten thousand years?" The DOE-paid scientists' position is absurd: as Senator Kerry of Nebraska said, "They lie a lot, the Department of Energy." Of course, they do. It's all very interesting . . . .

It finally dawned on us that the federal government was fronting for an extravagantly profitable private industry! It isn't tax dollars, but utility dollars that pay for every bit of what's going on. Congress is permitting itself to be used and financed by a private industry to promote what they call a "federal" project. Well, Congress may let itself be used in this fashion, but Nevada doesn't necessarily have to be its victim. Unfortunately, some people see all this money floating around, and they get in line. No vote our commission has ever taken on the dump has been unanimous — every one has been five to two against it, and the two members who are for it wonder about the rest of us. They think Nevada should deal with the federal government, with the Department of Energy, with the utilities; they recommend that we accept the dump and get what we can.

Our commission began recommending to the governor and the legislature certain actions to protect Nevada. Governor Miller has been terrific; and so have Senators Bryan and Reid, and Congressmen Bilbray and Vucanovich. The state legislature has enacted legislation that our commission proposed, virtually every county in the state has passed a resolution against the dump, and most (not all) elected officials have been publicly opposed to it. We have a pretty strongly unified voice in Nevada. If we can sustain that unity, it will be very hard for the government to force this project on a state that just will not take it.

Nevada may be a wilderness, as Senator Johnson would have it, but there are a million people here who have a lot of pride, and we're not going to be patsies for the federal government; nor will we suffer for the mistakes that the utility companies have made over the years. We had nothing to do with the mess they find themselves in. We are not involved in it, and we are not going to become a dumping ground for money-making private industries. And now we know that we're not just talking about domestic radioactivity: last year DOE blithely announced that they had forgotten to tell us that it won't be waste from American industry alone; they also plan to accept international waste, because there is no other repository anywhere in the world. Other developed countries have said to their own citizens, "We want to bury our radioactive waste near your community," but the people in those communities have gotten up in arms and will not permit it. I suspect that the bottom line on all this is that if Yucca Mountain ever gets established, Nevada will become the world's nuclear dump.

I have been intensely interested in this fight, and I will be a part of it till the end, if it is resolved in my lifetime. It may not be. Whether we have the guts, the intelligence, and the skill to defeat this federal onslaught, I don't know . . . but it would be a disgrace if we didn't try. To win will require a lot of conviction on the part of Nevadans who love this state. I am convinced that we can do it if we can keep enough people from being bought out; if we aren't sold down the river, we will get it stopped.

With over 80 percent of its area under the administration of the United States government, Nevada is really a federal preserve, and we can do little about it except to keep pecking away at picking up what land we need to continue our growth and development. To this end, I supported the "Sagebrush Rebellion," even though as a practical matter I was sure it was not going to work.[2] At least it brought our situation to the attention of the rest of the country, and particularly to eastern congressmen who don't care that we're sitting out here without control over our own lands. Very few easterners understand that when some of the western states came into the Union they were just given a blink and a nod and nothing else, because eastern states weren't affected that way. The Sagebrush Rebellion was a dramatic reminder that there is something different about the West that needs to be corrected; but I was under no illusion that Congress was going to make radical changes.

Land is necessary to the economic growth of Nevada, and it should belong to our citizens. Yet the federal government holds title to most of it, and they charge us to use it. That is unfair and improper — in effect, they rent public land to cattle and sheep people rather than turn it over to them and let them put it to maximum use. I'm not saying turn over all federal lands to the state of Nevada, but since the state needs land and can put it to productive use, it should be made available. There should be a way for title to those properties to be transferred to the state, which could either retain ownership or sell to private citizens, some of whose families have been using the land for generations, anyway.

The issue of control over Columbia River water really needs to be resolved. In fairness, why should millions of acre feet from the Columbia be allowed to flow into the ocean every year when there are nearby states that could make good use of that water? At some point people are going to have to sit down and forget their egos, restrain their greed, and begin to put that water to its most beneficial use in the West, not just in their respective states.

Most western governors are preoccupied with water. In California, Arizona, New Mexico, Nevada, Utah, and Colorado to some extent, it's an omnipresent problem. You have great dreams for your state to grow in population and productivity, but when you look down the pipe and see no water, you are *literally* just a desert, and growth and progress have stopped. That prospect is currently being faced by southern Nevada — nobody is going to move an industry here, if five years from now they may not be able to get a water permit.

Former Secretary of the Interior Stewart Udall gave a talk last year in which he pointed out that Nevada consumes more water per person than any other state in the West, and that's a key factor in limiting our chances for receiving additional water from the Colorado River. Until such time as we show that we're making the wisest, most efficient use of what's currently available to us, any hope of getting more water through the Colorado River Commission, or the Interior Department, is out the window. But we have not been frugal with it; particularly in southern Nevada, water waste is almost criminal! For some reason southern Clark Countians have decided that they want to live in a Shangri La, forgetting that this is a desert and that water should be used in that context. And Las Vegas is not alone in its tendency to self-delusion. For years Reno hasn't had enough water, and everybody understands that; but anybody who espouses water meters is political dead meat in Reno. It's absolutely ridiculous! They're all complaining about the limited reserves of water, but they won't conserve, won't do the things that should be done to make better use of the water they have. And they violently oppose putting a meter at the point of water use. I guess that's a typical human reaction.

Currently, Clark County has a plan — known as the Big Plan — to tap the water resources of neighboring counties, knowing full well that this will lower the water table in those counties. But water, as a general rule, is recognized as a state rather than a county resource — the mere presence of water in a county does not give that county control over it. No matter where it's located, I believe there's a state obligation to make the best use of all water in Nevada, and to put it where it's needed most. The state engineer is going to have to answer the question, "Is this county's water being wasted?" If it is not being used or appropriated, then there will be demands that it should be allocated elsewhere.

There is merit in that thinking, but the politics of the thing are quite something else. Small counties feel proprietary: "This water is in our county; this water belongs to us. Like the state of Oregon, we're not going to let Clark County or anybody else take our water, even though we're not using it." That attitude creates a serious political problem for anyone running for office, particularly a candidate for governor. If a candidate favors the interpretation that water is a state resource, he immediately loses every little county in the state because he's "permitting the big guy to steal from the little guys." So I would not expect to see any of our elected state officials take a position on this matter at all. Even the state engineer is part of an administration, and whatever decision he reaches affects the governor politically. If you are the governor, you hope that no decision will be made until your time is up; but it is something over which you have little control because it is a matter of law and evidence.

W̲ater or no water, in this day and age I doubt that we need another five or six major new hotels. I am not necessarily suggesting a slow-growth or no-growth policy, but we have to recognize that we're running into serious infrastructure problems in southern Nevada, where we cannot even keep up with the traffic. We had better be very careful about accepting any massive new developments, with the water and other services that they require.

Recently a plan was put forward to transform downtown Las Vegas into another Venice. Deteriorating for a number of years, downtown badly needs some imaginative redevelopment, but turning it into a pseudo-Venice initially struck me as absurd, particularly in light of our acknowledged shortage of water. Now I'm told we're not really talking about water, here; we are talking about something called "gray water," which is said to be currently unused, and of no use. In the Venetian scheme, this gray water would flow through canals to be constructed along Fremont Street. Steve Wynn apparently had some serious engineering done on this proposal, and he pretty well sold it to most of the people on Fremont Street. I've seen drawings, and they look appealing . . . and when I'm told that this use of the resource will not in any way affect other consumers of water in Las Vegas, I don't question it. I am among the large crowd of people in southern Nevada who are not about to second-guess Steve Wynn, who has come up before with seemingly radical ideas that have worked.

16

---

making the system
work

I have long been a
member of the NAACP, and have been reasonably active in
it here in southern Nevada. Our society should be an
integrated one, not segregated on the basis of race or color or
creed, and we ought to try to make opportunity in America
as equal as it can possibly be. By the early 1960s the country
was finally moving in that direction — at least I hoped that
was the situation — but we had all been so comfortable
during the Eisenhower presidency, with everybody kind of
going along to get along. America needs people who aren't
just following the mob all the time and doing what everybody
else is doing, and by keeping the pressure on, the NAACP has
been an effective agent for racial justice and for protecting the
constitutional rights of America's black citizens.

The Constitution is the bedrock of government in this country, and it must be zealously guarded against efforts to subvert any part of it. J. Edgar Hoover was just one of its enemies. The executive branch often smiles its way through abuses of the Constitution, and the courts sometimes abandon constitutional principles . . . and when the Supreme Court violates the Constitution, there's not much we can do about it! Even congress, in my opinion, occasionally passes unconstitutional laws — the selection of Yucca Mountain as the only site to be studied for the nuclear dump is unconstitutional, because it attacks states' rights. Are there any states' rights? The Constitution establishes and protects them; and if the lower courts say they don't exist, and the Supreme Court says there aren't any, then our court system is falling into the trap of saying, "Well, the only constitutional rights are those that are convenient to the federal government." We must have somebody who's willing to say, "No, look: you're wrong. You're missing the point. You're weakening the foundation of this country." I'm happy that there's an organization like the ACLU around that will stand up and fight!

I am a member of the ACLU, and occasionally I get letters from people who brand me as a communist or something because the ACLU is defending the rights of Nazis to march. I write back and tell them that I'm an arch-conservative: I believe in the Constitution of the United States; I believe in the Bill of Rights. People are entitled to express their views in this country . . . whether their views are consistent with mine or not is totally immaterial, they have that right. So I tell them, "Shame on you for degrading the Constitution of the United States!" which, I must say, they usually don't find to be an acceptable response. [laughter] Even my wife gets very annoyed at some of the things that the ACLU does . . . but that's not the point. The point is that here's a group that says, "This country was founded on certain fundamental principles, and it's the principles that are important, not any particular expression of them." If we're not willing to stand or fall on those principles, we've lost the ball game; and if we decide that all Americans have to be "politically correct" or socially correct, then we miss the whole point!

I've taken some heat on this, but so what? I don't always agree with what the ACLU does, either, but they are standing up for the rights of American citizens, and they're willing to go to court to fight for those rights, even though some of the cases they must accept to do it are repugnant. I appreciate that, and I am happy to be a part of it.

I look upon the election of regents somewhat as I look on judgeships — the board of regents of the university system should be people who are highly qualified with good backgrounds in education; people who have standing in the communities. The mere fact that a person can win an election, in my opinion, shouldn't necessarily qualify him or her to be a regent of the University of Nevada. Instead, I would prefer to rely on the judgment of a governor (or a governor with approval of the state senate) in appointing people that are qualified, and appointing them for much longer terms. The University of California system, for example, appoints regents for twelve years. They are all outstanding people whose judgment is not questioned, and they haven't had to get out, run around and collect the money and do all the unsavory things that you have to do in a campaign. I still think that is the best system, and so I hope that ultimately we will not only appoint regents but also judges, as is done in many other states. These people could go through a confirmation process following the appointment.

The danger in electing regents rather than appointing them derives from the process of campaigning: you want to collect money to be successful, and when you do that you are subject to the pressures of special interest groups which will continue after the election and while you are serving. An example is the current competition between the two University of Nevada campuses: if your jurisdiction is southern Nevada, and you are to run successfully there, you want to come home to the people and tell them about all the "pork" that you got for UNLV. The same thing is true with UNR and the people who run from the northern part of the state. This isn't necessarily the best goal of government for a university system, and bringing home the pork shouldn't be the criterion for holding the office of regent. The university system is for the whole state, and its needs should be viewed impartially and objectively. That's just one of the dangers of the system we presently have.

The argument that the people should have the final say over who holds office is a very appealing argument, but it doesn't necessarily lead to the best governing of a particular body. Where judges are elected, they have to continue to campaign while they're on the bench until their next election. If the labor unions or whoever supported them appears before them in a case . . . there are all of those pressures which appointments would alleviate to a considerable extent. The same with regents. If they are appointed, they wouldn't have to appear at every basketball game and every parade and everything else. There would not be this continuous, never-ending campaign for reelection the next time. As a consequence, I think that they could do a more efficient job of administering the affairs of the university system of Nevada, not worrying so much about whether people think they're great guys.

Under our political system, in order to become a United States Senator you have to have something on the ball. Occasionally a flake or somebody who really shouldn't be there makes it to Washington, but in general I have a lot of confidence in the Senate and a high regard for senators. I don't feel that way about our state legislature, though. A state legislator is often beholden to a narrow constituency for his election, and he often has little or no concern about broader issues, so in the capitol building you see a great many special interests being strongly represented. Bette and I both used to say, "Well, you know, we get what we deserve here. These people pretty-well represent the people in their districts." That isn't saying much for the districts in many cases . . . . [laughter] Sometimes the governor and the legislators don't even talk the same political language. A governor generally will not wheel and deal like a legislator; he will not stoop to trading gaming licenses for political favors, or any of the other things that some legislators sometimes do. But he must find *some* way to deal with these special-interest pleaders, some of questionable integrity, who historically populate the Nevada capitol.

Generally speaking, people elected to the state legislature can be easily swayed in the wrong direction if they don't get strong leadership, and this is at least partially due to a flaw in Nevada's system of government. Our legislature meets only biennially, so when it is in session legislators have to jam a lot of things in, and they get caught in a time crunch. Unless you have a few good, solid people who can move that herd in the right direction, you can be in real trouble! (Another factor affecting their behavior may be that state legislators are given much less attention than people in higher office — the lower you are on the scale, the less public scrutiny there is.)

Only those people who haven't succumbed to the pressure to trade votes and deal for political favors have become outstanding state legislators in Nevada. They survived over long periods of time and compiled creditable records because they established reputations for responsibility and trustworthiness that other people did not. You can pick out maybe eight or ten legislators in the history of this state who have been outstanding. They had in common that they were all people of great integrity.

Being governor of Nevada was exhilarating. It was all pretty heady business. You have a lot of people telling you what a great guy you are; how they don't understand how the state ever managed to survive until you got there. If you start to believe any of that, then it becomes a real threat to you and the office you hold. When I was elected, for the first time in our lives my wife and I experienced walking into rooms where everybody was pawing, grabbing, and asking for our autographs. Most of the people, we didn't even know. And you listen to that stuff for a while, and you begin to think, "Gee, I didn't realize how great I am until now." You have to have some kind of a sense of balance about it or it will destroy you. Fortunately, after you experience this for a while it begins to wear off, and I always understood who I was, and where I was coming from: I wasn't some great guy. Part of the proof of that to me is that when I left office, I really didn't miss any of it.

The first time I was elected I had such a substantial margin of victory that I thought I could say, "OK, everybody loves me. Now let's all go on and accomplish a lot of things." But I soon learned that my emphatic victory carried very little influence, particularly in the legislature. Legislators are independent, and they were not at all impressed — they pretty well did what they wanted, and what historically they could be expected to do. Not only did my sizeable victory bring me no influence with the legislature, I found that some situations would probably have gone better had I stayed out of the debate. Hence my disappointment in the progress of my civil rights agenda, which took several years to get into any kind of workable shape. You know the old maxim about somebody coming along and asking you for your support, and you say, "I will be against you or for you, whichever will do you the most good . . . ? " Well, I know that sometimes my being against something improved its chances. [laughter]

People have some inflated notions of what it's like to be governor of the state. It is not the be-all, end-all that it is cracked up to be, not by any means. The truth is, it's a mad scramble from the day you are elected until the day you get out — you face one crisis after another with your appointees, your programs, the media, and the opposing political party. And I learned that anything you do that steps on the toes of "big" people is going to bring a lot of flak. That they like you personally will not keep them from doing everything they can to get you out of office if they don't think you're acting in their best interests . . . . But I actually enjoyed being challenged on positions that I felt strongly about. It was fun to play that game and see if you could win, and I discovered that although you don't carry the day nearly as often as you think you should, if you keep plugging away you can get some satisfaction in the end.

Although I used to feel sorry for myself when the press and the special interests were after me, things are much worse for elected officials now. I don't envy any of these folks who wake up every morning to open a newspaper and read what is being said about them today. You live your life running, looking for shadows, and worrying about who's going to accuse you of something next; and how to counter it, and how you can survive in office, and do you have enough money for the next election, and . . . . It's a hell of a way to live! We are fortunate that there are a few strong, able, intelligent people who are willing to accept the rigors and dangers of public life in order to serve their state and nation. I would never discourage anyone from running. If you never run, you never win.

Appendix

the sam giancana incident: frank sinatra loses his nevada gaming license

Between 1967 and 1969 Mary Ellen Glass, then the director of the University of Nevada's Oral History Program, recorded the life history of Edward A. Olsen, who was chairman of the Nevada Gaming Commission at the time of the events described on pages 93-94. In typescript form Mr. Olsen's oral history is in the archive of the Oral History Program, and copies of the work have been acquired by the University of Nevada Libraries in Reno and Las Vegas. The following is reproduced from pages 385-394 of Olsen's oral history:

It was on a Saturday afternoon, the day before Labor Day, and I was in my office in Carson when Mr. Sinatra's accountant called me; Mr. Newell Hancock was his accountant. And Mr. Hancock said that Mr. Sinatra was upset about the publicity. He felt that I had initiated the publicity through issuance of subpoenas, which was absolutely incorrect, because no one except the recipients of the subpoenas even had knowledge of it at that point.

Mr. Hancock suggested that Mr. Sinatra had advanced the thought that perhaps I should come up and have dinner with him and catch the show that night. And I told Mr. Hancock that under the circumstances I didn't really think that that was the best idea. And Hancock says, "Well, he wants to meet with you."

And I said, "Well, that's fine. I will meet with him any time, but it will be in my office."

Well, he was afraid that there would be a lot of press and photographers there. It was a Saturday afternoon, the building's locked, and there's absolutely nobody around the place except my own people.

So then, we weren't making any headway, and Hancock, who lived at the lake — has a summer home at the lake, finally asked if — well, would I be willing to meet with Sinatra on neutral territory, such as his home.

And I understood Sinatra's desire to avoid personal confrontation with the press of some kind, because he'd probably get into a brawl with them. So I did agree. I said yes, I'd be willing to discuss the matter with Sinatra at Hancock's home, but that really, I saw no point to it because Sinatra and I had already discussed this and we were still trying to get the facts of the thing and we weren't having too much success. So that was the end of that conversation.

It was about thirty minutes later that the phone rings again and a very abrupt feminine voice inquires for me and advises me to please hold the line for Mr. Sinatra. Mr. Sinatra came on and — quite charming — and he wanted to know if I wouldn't come up and join him for dinner and catch the show.

And I told him that I had already declined that gracious invitation extended though Mr. Hancock, and he said, "Why?" Well, he wanted to talk to me. I suggested again that he come to the office. And he likewise brought up the point that the newspaper and the press and everything were around there.

I'm not going to continue any further with this conversation at the moment because I did write a memorandum on it at the time which I don't appear to have a copy of at the moment. I'm sure I can show you the one in the state file if necessary. And I think it would probably be better if I refreshed my recollection upon that. It was a classic conversation. It was just — [laughing]. And Mr. Hancock subsequently said that he kicked himself all over the lot for ever giving Sinatra my telephone number [laughing].

In the course of the conversation — just briefly to summarize — there were, oh, a number of things that just could not be ignored said and, I'm certain, did play a part in what decision ultimately was made in this thing.

This is the memorandum I wrote for the files on September 4, 1963, trying to recap that hectic Labor Day weekend. (It is interesting to note how only nine years ago language which today is commonplace on protest signs, in magazines, et cetera, was sealed in large envelopes and labeled "obscene" to protect the pristine eyes of young women file clerks.)

OBSCENE OBSCENE
CONFIDENTIAL CONFIDENTIAL

September 4, 1963

Memo Gaming Control Board:

Re: Frank Sinatra
Sam Giancana

The following incidents and conversations which occurred on August 29, 30 and 31 and September 1 and 2, 1963, are recounted here to the best of my memory and knowledge.

On August 29, during the evening hours at his home, Jack Stratton, office manager for the Board, received a telephone call from William Sinnott, a former member of the Board who now appears to be occasionally employed in a reportorial capacity by the *Las Vegas Sun*. Mr. Sinnott requested information in connection with a newspaper story which appeared in early August or late July in the *Chicago Sun-Times*, under the by-line of Sandy Smith. The story reported a visit to Cal-Neva Lodge, of which Mr. Sinatra is the principal gaming licensee, of Giancana on two occasions during late July. The story told of an alleged altercation between Giancana and an unnamed individual and said Sinatra broke up the fight after Eddie King, Cal-Neva's maitre d', had become involved. The story added that Nevada gaming authorities were investigating the matter to determine if the Cal-Neva gaming licensee had violated Nevada's regulation against catering to persons of nationally notorious and unsavory repute. Giancana unquestionably holds such a reputation and has been listed in the Nevada "black book" since its inception. Mr. Stratton had no knowledge of the Chicago story or of the fact that Giancana's visit had been under intensive investigation by the Board since about July 28. Thus, Stratton was unable to provide any information to Sinnott. Sinnott did not call the chairman or a member of the Board. The *Las Vegas Sun* printed liberal excerpts from the Chicago story in its Friday morning edition of August 30.

Later that day, August 30, Dwight Dyer of KCRL-TV, Reno, telephoned the chairman of the Board to enquire about the Chicago story. He was told the matter had been under investigation since its inception; that a number of persons at the ownership, managerial and employee levels of Cal-Neva had been interviewed; and that the investigation could not be concluded until certain discrepancies in the information provided could be resolved.

Why it took almost a month for the Chicago story (another along the same line had subsequently appeared in the *Washington News*) to come to light in Nevada is a continuing mystery of the newspaper business. Suffice to say, I was besieged with telephone calls from wire services and newspapers from various parts of the country after Mr. Dyer's television program appeared. The same statements given Dyer were repeated to all other callers. The Board does not make a practice of publicizing its investigative proceedings, but it would have been manifestly ridiculous to deny such an investigation was under way when the matter first came to public light in Chicago, then in Washington and belatedly in the Nevada press.

It is felt the foregoing, although lengthy and essentially trivial, is necessary for the reader to put the balance of this report in perspective.

(The information developed during the Giancana investigation is the subject of other memoranda and transcripts and is touched upon in this report only when required for clarification.)

About 3:30 p.m., Saturday, August 31, while at the office on other matters, I received a telephone call from Newell Hancock, an original member of the Board and for the last several years a partner in the firm of Certified Public Accountants which represents Cal-Neva Lodge in a number of capacities.

Mr. Hancock opened the conversation with: "Ed, what in the hell are you doing to us with all this publicity?" I explained to Hancock that the publicity did not originate with the Board, but developed in the manner set forth in the foregoing portion of this memorandum.

Hancock went on to say that "Frank is irritated" and would like to meet with me to discuss the matter, with the aim of making a statement to counteract the publicity. He asked me to come up to Cal-Neva and discuss the matter with Mr. Sinatra, then stay for the dinner show of which he and Dean Martin were the stars. I replied that I felt this would be inappropriate under the circumstances and added that since Mr. Sinatra wished to see me, it would be better for such a meeting to be held in my office in the presence of others, including my secretary who would make a record of the conversation. I also suggested that Mr. Sinatra bring with him such personnel as could perhaps resolve the conflicts in statements made earlier by Mr. Sinatra, Mr. King and others interviewed.

(It should be noted here that Mr. King freely gave a statement to a Board agent at the inception of the investigation, but when appearing under subpoena August 30, "respectfully declined" to answer any questions under oath pending consultation with an attorney. I had been informed a few minutes before King's appearance by the attorney for Cal-Neva that King might have reason to fear a state criminal charge of obstructing justice if he testified under oath. His subpoena was extended to September 10.)

Returning to the conversation with Hancock, he asked if I would be available over the Labor Day weekend. I said I would be available at my office at Mr. Sinatra's convenience. Hancock suggested 3:30 p.m. Sunday, September 1, to which I acquiesced.

Within one-half hour, about 4 p.m., my telephone rang again. It was Mr. Sinatra. To describe him as "irritated" was a masterful understatement. He was infuriated.

He asked why I couldn't come up to the Cal-Neva to see him. I gave him the same reasons as I had given Hancock. To which he replied, "You're acting like a fucking cop . . . I just want to talk to you off the record."

I asked him why he couldn't just as easily come to my office. He indicated he didn't wish to encounter reporters. As I started to assure him such would not be the case, he said in essence: "Listen, Ed, I haven't had to take this kind of shit from anybody in the country and I'm not going to take it from you people."

He continued: "I want you to come up here and have dinner with me . . . and bring that shit heel friend, La France." (Mr. La France is the chief of the Board's investigative division and has participated in some of the interviews mentioned earlier.)

At this point, seeing that the conversation was becoming exceptionally enlightening, I motioned to Mr. La France and Guy Farmer, assistant executive secretary of the Gaming Commission, the only other persons in the office, to pick up extensions of my telephone line.

Mr. Sinatra went on to say: "It's you and your God damn subpoenas which have caused all this trouble." I replied that only the Board and the people subpoenaed the day before were aware of the subpoenas. "You are a God damn liar . . . it's all over the papers," he said. I said the subpoenas were not in the papers. He said they were. I said they were not. He said "I'll bet you $50,000." I said, "I haven't got $50,000 to bet." He said, "You're not in the same class with me." I said, "I certainly hope not."

Mr. Sinatra continued: "All right I'm never coming to see you again. I came to see you in Las Vegas and if you had conducted this investigation like a gentleman and come up here to see my people instead of sending those God damn subpoenas, you would have gotten all the information you wanted."

I pointed out that I had indeed sent three agents and a stenographer to Cal-Neva Lodge to interview witnesses the same night Mr. Leypoldt and myself had interviewed Sinatra in Las Vegas. I noted that Mr. D'Amato had declined to be interviewed by our agents and that Mr. King had declined to be interviewed by our agents and that Mr. King obviously had lied. I added that I wasn't satisfied at this time that Sinatra himself had told us the truth.

He said what about? I said he denied breaking up the fight involving Giancana, while another witness said otherwise. (This witness said Sinatra applied a band-aid after Giancana and King combined forces to work him over in Phyllis McGuire's chalet at Cal-Neva Lodge.)

"I'm never coming to see you again," said Sinatra. I told him if I wanted to see him I would send a subpoena.

"You just try and find me," he said. "And if you do, you can look for a big, fat surprise . . . a big, fat, fucking surprise. You remember that. Now listen to me, Ed . . . Don't fuck with me. Don't fuck with me. Just don't fuck with me."

The tone of his voice was menacing and I asked, "Are you threatening me?" He replied, "No . . . just don't fuck with me." . . . "And you can tell that to your fucking Board and that fucking Commission, too."

Repeatedly, during the conversation, I suggested to Mr. Sinatra that he hang up and call me back another time when he was not so emotionally overwrought.

This suggestion only seemed to make him angrier. He noted that he has other enterprises from which he makes his living, that Cal-Neva is only incidental to his welfare but is important to the livelihoods of many "little people."

I suggested it might be better for all concerned if he concentrated on his enterprises elsewhere and departed the Nevada gambling scene.

He replied, "I might just do that . . . and when I do, I'm going to tell the world what a bunch of fucking idiots run things in this state."

At this point he renewed his invitation to me and my friends to come up for dinner. I refused the invitation. "You just think about it," he said.

The conversation ended at this point. I detected no indication during the conversation that Mr. Sinatra might have been drinking. He appeared on his show a few hours later that evening.

Upon returning to my home, I received another call from Mr. Hancock about 5:30 p.m. enquiring if I had received a call from Sinatra. I told him yes and relayed a brief sample of the dialogue. Hancock appeared stunned and commented, "Well, I may have just blown a client." He explained that when he had called Sinatra to suggest the 3:30 p.m. Sunday appointment in my office, Sinatra had expressed extreme displeasure and asked for my telephone number. Hancock complied and hadn't heard from Sinatra since.

However, Hancock had heard from D'Amato who reported that two Board agents had arrived at the Lodge to observe the 6 p.m. count of gambling table drop boxes. (This is a routine Board program and has been conducted on Labor Day weekend in the Lake Tahoe area for the past three summers. The Cal-Neva schedule had been set up well in advance, but had slipped my mind, and it was merely coincidence that the two agents arrived within minutes after

Sinatra hung up the phone to me.) Hancock said he advised D'Amato it was just a routine program and to think nothing of it. He said D'Amato was upset, however, because when he advised Sinatra of the agents' presence, Sinatra had said: "Throw the dirty sons of bitches out of the house." Sinatra also ordered that if the agents returned, he was to be personally notified. The agents had no knowledge of the preceding information or of my talk with Sinatra. It developed there was no trouble because Irving Pearleman, the casino manager, advised them on arrival that the count already had begun, so the agents concluded there was no point in entering the counting room at that time. They advised Pearleman they would return another time. He asked if they would be back Sunday, and they said no because they had other clubs scheduled for that day. (Actually, the agents had previously been instructed to avoid Cal-Neva Sunday because we had another undercover counting program underway there that day. This program likewise is routine and has been carried throughout the state.) The agents in the weekend box counting program at the Lake were Don Aikin and Gene Kramer of the audit division.

In keeping with their schedule, Aikin and Kramer appeared at Cal-Neva Monday (Labor Day) for the 6 a.m. count. Shortly before 9 a.m., Aikin awakened me by telephone at my home and reported he and Kramer wished to see me quickly. I told them to come over to the house immediately. They arrived about 9 a.m.

The two agents reported to me that at the completion of the count, which had been conducted in a friendly atmosphere, Mr. D'Amato had surreptitiously placed two $100 bills in the crook of Kramer's arm as he sat at the counting table. (Details of this matter are reported in another memorandum by the agents concerned.) Suffice to say here, the money was returned and D'Amato explained that it was just a little gift to compensate for the inconvenience caused them Saturday night. Of course, the agents had no knowledge of having been inconvenienced Saturday night since it was they who made the decision not to enter the counting room after being told the count already was underway.

It was indeed an interesting Labor Day weekend in Carson City.

Edward A. Olsen
Chairman

Notes

Preface

1. Governor Sawyer's private papers will be donated to the University of Nevada, Reno, where they will be housed in the Special Collections department of the Getchell Library. Formal transferral of the papers is planned for the fall of 1993. The state papers of all Nevada's governors are in the state archives in Carson City.

Chapter 3

1. In the 1950 Florida Democratic primary, George Smathers had defeated incumbent Senator Claude Pepper in a bruising contest in which he had accused Pepper of being soft on communism.

2. Beginning in 1950 Wisconsin Senator Joseph R. McCarthy, a Republican, became one of the most feared men in America by charging others with secretly being "card-carrying Communists," or with being sympathetic to the communist agenda. Although he never produced a shred of evidence to support his accusations, he wrecked the careers of a number of elected officials and bureaucrats, and ruined the lives of many Americans not in government, before the Senate finally censured him in 1954. McCarthy died of cirrhosis of the liver in 1957.

3. In 1950, Pat McCarran was elected to his fourth term in the U.S. Senate. When he died in September 1954, the Republicans argued that his appointed successor, Ernest Brown, should serve out the years remaining in McCarran's term. The Democrats contended that Brown's seat should be contested in the next general election, which was in November. The Nevada supreme court ruled in favor of the Democrats.

4. After winning the 1954 election to Pat McCarran's seat, Alan Bible served four terms as United States senator from Nevada: he completed Patrick McCarran's term, and went on to serve three consecutive terms, 1957-1974 before retiring. Following the election of Paul Laxalt to succeed him in 1974, Bible resigned before his term was up so that Laxalt could replace him and gain senatorial seniority.

5. Minard W. Stout was hired as president of the University of Nevada in 1952. As one of his first official acts he lowered entrance requirements so that any graduate of a Nevada high school was eligible for admission regardless of grades and class standing. Some professors at the university took exception to this and testified against the policy before the legislature. One of them, Frank Richardson, a biology professor, was subsequently fired by President Stout. A complicated legal struggle ensued, with Richardson eventually being reinstated by the Nevada supreme court. As Stout continued in his autocratic ways, the American Association of University Professors censured the university, there were student demonstrations against President Stout, and the 1955 legislature ordered a full investigation, which was headed by Dean E. McHenry of UCLA. McHenry recommended changes in the selection and composition of the board of regents, and further suggested that the board be enlarged from five to nine members. These recommendations were widely interpreted as being anti-Stout, since the board at that time was composed of people who supported him.

Chapter 4

1. Errett L. Cord was a wealthy businessman and manufacturer whose Cord automobiles of the 1930s, built in his home state of Indiana, were technological (and pricey) marvels. Cord was induced by Norman Biltz to move to Nevada to take advantage of the state's tax laws. He soon became an influential member of Pat McCarran's circle, and after McCarran's death Cord began advancing his own candidates for office.

2. Dr. Fred Anderson was a Reno surgeon, a university regent, and a prominent Democrat. A 1928 graduate of the University of Nevada, he had been a Rhodes Scholar before entering the Harvard School of Medicine, where he received his medical training.

3. Born in 1908, Hazel Erskine was one of the early members of Columbia University's Bureau of Applied Social Research, and after World War II she became editor of the "Polls" section of *Public Opinion Quarterly*. After marrying the architect Graham Erskine, she moved to Reno, and became an active advocate of a number of liberal political and social

causes. She was instrumental in making possible Grant Sawyer's successful campaign for governor in 1958. An "In Memoriam" article by George Rudiak and Ralph L. Denton (*Public Opinion Quarterly*, 1975-76, vol. 39, p. 574) states that:

> Hazel had spotted in Grant Sawyer, a young district attorney from rural Elko County, an astute and pragmatic politician who was at the same time a man of principle and "educable" — as Hazel put it — in the social and human needs of the state.
>
> Sawyer, at that time, had his eye on the post of state attorney general, and proved hesitant when Hazel sought to persuade him to run for governor. Hazel thereupon took it upon herself to visit all 17 counties of the sixth largest state in the union (geographically speaking) to drum up support and money for a Sawyer candidacy. She raised a campaign chest of $10,000 — which was a respectable start for a campaign fund in the pre-inflation era in a state with fewer than 150,000 voters. So well did she do her work that Sawyer was persuaded to run, was elected, and provided an enlightened administration for Nevada for two successive terms. Hazel was, moreover, a key campaign worker in both Sawyer campaigns, organizing, planning, pinpointing the issues, and always testing the political ozone with the techniques of her life's work — public opinion polling.

4. In the Democratic primary of 1958 Grant Sawyer received 20,711 votes. Harvey Dickerson got 13,372; George Franklin, 10,175; and William Pate, 473.

5. In the general election of 1958, 60 percent of the votes cast went to Grant Sawyer. He received 50,864 votes for governor, to Charles Russell's 34,025.

Chapter 5

1. Nevada's legislature met biennially. AB1 (January 19, 1959) amended the Nevada Revised Statutes to require annual meetings, those falling in odd-numbered years to be general sessions, and those in even-numbered years to be reserved for budget matters.

2. Democrat Maude Frazier served in the Nevada State Assembly from 1951 to 1962. Sympathetic to many of Gov. Sawyer's positions, she became his political ally. In 1962, when Lt. Gov. Rex Bell died in office, Sawyer appointed her to serve out Bell's term.

3. Nevada's Freeport Act, passed in 1949, provided tax incentives for the storage and maintenance of goods in interstate commerce. Amended several times by the legislature, in 1960 it was made part of the state constitution.

Chapter 6

1. SB170 (1955) provided for the regulation of gaming and the issuance, suspension and revocation of gaming licenses, enforced by a State Gaming Control Board under the authority of the Nevada Tax Commission.

2. AB144, effecting this change, was quickly passed by the 1959 legislature.

3. A rap sheet is a record of arrests and charges, which may or may not show convictions.

4. See: Marshall v. Sawyer, 301 F.2d, at 646 (1962); Marshall v. Sawyer, 365 F.2d, at 112 (1966); Marshall v. Sawyer, 385 U.S. 1006 (1967) cert. denied; Spilotro v. State, 99 Nev. 187, at 190 (1983)

5. For a comprehensive treatment of the constitutional issues surrounding Nevada's black book, see Michael W. Bowers and Dina Titus, "Nevada's Black Book: Protecting the State's Gaming Industry," *Whittier Law Review* (Nov. 1987).

Chapter 7

1. In 1947 President Truman's Committee on Civil Rights verified the pervasiveness of racial crimes of all types and the widespread denial of equal opportunities to black Americans. Truman's civil rights legislative package failed to pass, but in 1957 Congress established a Civil Rights Commission and a Civil Rights Division in the Department of Justice, both concerned primarily with protecting the voting rights of all citizens. It was not until 1964 that a comprehensive Civil Rights Act was passed which forbade discrimination in all places of public accommodation.

2. In 1960, presidential candidate John F. Kennedy would only go as far as advocating moral leadership on the issue of civil rights.

3. NGC Regulation 5.011.

4. Officially known as the Nevada Commission on Equal Rights of Citizens, NRS233.010.

5. Storey County's James M. Slattery (Republican) served nine terms in the Nevada State Senate, 1955-1970. As recorded on p. 451 of the *Journal of the Senate* for the 52nd session (1963), Slattery remarked: "I feel that the colored people in this state have never been so well off. We have looked into the situation in Las Vegas — they are living in fine homes (their houses are better than mine) and they are driving fine big cars (I have a beat-up old Chevrolet) . . . . "

6. See *Nevada Public Affairs Review*, 1987, No. 2. Contributions by Leslie B. Gray and Elmer R. Rusco suggest that Governor Sawyer may not always have exerted the full power of his office in attacking racial discrimination in the state. It should be noted, however, that Rusco also writes that Sawyer "was courageous in advocating and working for civil rights legislation throughout his eight years as governor." (p. 76)

7. A Las Vegas neighborhood, by the mid 1940s the Westside had become home to many southern blacks drawn to Clark County to work in defense industries. It is the largest black community in Nevada.

8. After passage of the 1964 national Civil Rights Act banning discrimination in employment and accommodations, the Nevada legislature passed an almost identical civil rights bill. On April 5, 1965, Governor Sawyer signed the bill into law.

Chapter 8

1. George Whittell originally purchased 10,000 acres abutting the Lake Tahoe shore in 1936. In 1971, much of the Whittell estate was purchased by New York financier Jack J. Dreyfus, who later sold all but 141 acres to the federal government.

2. In 1965 Sen. Alan Bible introduced legislation to fund the Southern Nevada Water Project. Passed in 1966, the project provided for the construction of mains to carry 132,000 acre feet of water annually from Lake Mead to Clark County, finally delivering to Nevada its full legal share of Colorado River water.

3. In 1952, Arizona filed suit against California in federal court, claiming that California was consuming more water than it was entitled to under the provisions of the 1922 Colorado River Compact. Nevada asked for permission to intervene in the suit to protect its water rights. Hugh Shamberger, Nevada's state engineer, calculated that by the year 2000, Nevada's water needs would exceed 500,000 acre feet per year, and that was the volume requested by former state attorney general Alan Bible when he argued Nevada's case before the high court.

4. The move to establish the Great Basin National Park began in 1957. In 1959, Senator Alan Bible proposed the creation of a 147,000 acre national park for the Wheeler Peak area in eastern Nevada. Representative Walter Baring countered with a plan that included only about 47,000 acres. When the park was finally established in 1986 it encompassed about 72,000 acres.

5. The Multiple Use-Sustained Yield Act specifies that National Forest lands shall be administered for outdoor recreation, range, timber, watershed, etc., "in such combination and manner that they will best meet and serve human needs."

Chapter 9

1. In the 1964 U.S. Senate race, Paul Laxalt lost to Howard Cannon by only forty-eight votes.

2. Flora Dungan (Democrat) served two terms as Clark County representative in the Nevada State Assembly, 1963-64 and 1967-68. She and Clare Woodbury, another Las Vegas resident, brought a federal suit to force Nevada to observe the one-man, one-vote rule, thus giving Clark and Washoe counties combined 81 percent of Nevada's senators and assemblymen.

3. In 1965 Governor Sawyer was also elected chairman of the Western Governors' Conference. This was the first time that the same man had been chairman of the national and western conferences of governors simultaneously.

4. In the 1988 presidential campaign the Republican party ran a television spot attacking the Democratic candidate, Massachusetts Governor Michael Dukakis. Featuring the visage of Willie Horton — a black convicted felon who committed other crimes while on furlough from the Massachusetts state prison — the ad clearly implied that Dukakis coddled criminals; it was also perceived as racist by many commentators.

Chapter 10

1. The Average Day's Attendance in Nevada public schools increased by 87 percent from school year 1958-59 to 1965-66. State support per pupil during that same period rose 187 percent, and teachers' salaries went up by 35 percent. Simultaneously, university enrollment increased by 116 percent, and professors' salaries grew by 42 percent.

2. In the 1966 general election Grant Sawyer received 65,870 votes for governor, to Paul Laxalt's 71,807.

Chapter 13

1. The *Las Vegas Sun* reported that Johnson received 6 1/2 votes; Kennedy, 5 1/2; Stevenson, 2 1/2; and Symington, 1/2.

2. D. N. "Mike" O'Callaghan, a Democrat, served two terms as governor of Nevada, 1971-1978.

3. James Santini served four terms in Congress, 1975-1982.

4. In the end, Bryan won by over 14,000 votes, 175,548 to 161,336.

5. S. 279, introduced in 1991, was popularly known as CAFE (Corporate Average Fuel Economy) legislation. It would have addressed a variety of environmental and economic concerns by requiring improved fuel economy in motor vehicles sold in the United States. Although Sen. Bryan's bill was defeated by three votes, CAFE legislation may be reintroduced during the Clinton administration.

6. PL101-618, known as the Fallon Paiute-Shoshone Tribal Settlement Act, passed Nov. 16, 1990. Part II of the act specifies the equitable apportionment of water flowing from Lake Tahoe to Pyramid Lake via the Truckee River.

7. Shortly after List's election victory in 1978, it was revealed by the *Las Vegas Sun* that he was being investigated by the State Gaming Control Board. List was said to have offered to use his influence as governor (if elected) with the State Gaming Commission on behalf of Frank Rosenthal, in return for suppression prior to the election of information that List had, while he was Nevada's attorney general, accepted complimentary rooms, meals, telephone calls, etc. from the Stardust Hotel-Casino. In the end, nothing came of the investigation.

Chapter 14

1. Harry Truman got his start under the sponsorship of Boss Thomas J. Pendergast, who controlled Democratic politics in Kansas City, Mo., for thirty years. In 1939 Pendergast was convicted of income tax evasion and sent to Leavenworth prison. He was shortly paroled on condition that he stay out of politics for five years.

2. In 1946 Richard Nixon ran for Congress in the 12th district of California against Democrat Jerry Voorhis. Nixon's allegation that Voorhis harbored communist sympathies became a key point in his campaign, and in Congress he went on to lead the investigation of Alger Hiss as a communist infiltrator of the U.S. government. In 1950 Nixon defeated Democrat Helen Gahagan Douglas for the U.S. Senate in a dirty campaign again featuring charges of communism. Through his actions Richard Nixon had earned the contempt of Democrats, who widely perceived him to be a liar and a "red baiter."

Chapter 15

1. The Nevada Commission on Nuclear Projects was formed on January 29, 1985.

2. "Sagebrush Rebellion" was the name given to a movement begun by Elko County livestock owners in protest of the Federal Lands Policy and Management Act of 1976. As it gained momentum, the movement's leaders called for the government to turn over to Nevada almost 50 million acres of federally-administered land in the state, and this demand received support from agriculturalists and mining interests throughout the West. In 1979 the state legislature was persuaded to bring suit against the United States in the cause of the "rebellion," but the suit failed.

Index

Philippine Civil Affairs Unit
  (PCAU), 26
Pierce, Ann, 212
Pittman, Key, 182
PL101-618, (Fallon Paiute-
  Shoshone Tribal Settle-
  ment Act, 1990), 244
Pribbernow, Carlisle, 30
Public Opinion Quarterly,
  240, 241
Puccinelli, Alex, 40
Puccinelli, Leo, 41

Q

Quayle, Dan, 209

R

Raggio, Bill, 128
Reagan, Ronald, 183, 206,
  207-208
Reid, Harry, 24, 180-182, 214
Reno Gazette, 77-78
Reynolds v. *Sims* (1964), 121
Richardson, Frank, 240
Robbins, Jack, 43, 49
Rockefeller, Nelson, 74
Roosevelt, Eleanor, 189, 195,
  205-206
Roosevelt, Franklin D., 187-
  188, 195
Rosenthal, Frank, 244
Rudiak, George, 241
Rusco, Elmer R., 242

Russell, Charles, 49, 52, 53,
  58, 60, 63, 64, 69, 73, 81,
  84, 129, 154-155, 241
Ryan, Jim "Sailor," 48, 56

S

S. 279. *See* Corporate Average Fuel Economy bill
"Sagebrush Rebellion," 216,
  245
Salinger, Pierre, 191
Santini, Jim, 175-176, 244
Sawyer, Bette N., 30-31, 38,
  43, 59, 70, 73, 74, 160,
  161, 163, 189, 191
Sawyer, Byrd Fanita (née
  Wall), 6-7
Sawyer, Frank Grant:
  ancestors/family, 3-13, 15,
  17-18, 153-159; childhood/
  youth, 5-21; and civil
  rights, 95-106; education,
  9-10, 13-21, 23-25, 31-32;
  as Elko County DA, 41-47;
  and gaming regulation, 81-
  94; as governor, 53-64, 67-
  80, 81-94, 95-106, 107-115,
  117-132, 133-139, 159-161,
  211-219; marriage/family,
  30-31, 39, 160-163; and
  military service, 25-35; as
  University of Nevada
  regent, 51-52, 223-224
Sawyer, Gail, 16, 30, 47,
  160-163

Photo
Credits

Evelyn Roen and Grant Saw-
yer: *Courtesy Grant Sawyer*; Harry William Sawyer: *Courtesy Nevada
Historical Society*; Byrd Sawyer: *Courtesy Churchill County Museum*; Patrick
A. McCarran: *Courtesy UNLV Special Collections, Elbert Edwards Collection*;
Grant Sawyer, 1945: *Courtesy Grant Sawyer*; Elko little theater production:
Courtesy UNR Special Collections; Gail Sawyer: *Courtesy The Northeastern
Nevada Museum*; Grant Sawyer, 1960: *Courtesy UNR Special Collections*;
Marilyn Monroe and Frank Sinatra: *Courtesy* Dateline: Reno, *by
Dondero/Stoess*; Civil rights meeting: *Courtesy Nevada State Library and
Archives*; Picketing protestors: *Courtesy UNR Special Collections*; Edmund
Brown and Grant Sawyer: *Courtesy Grant Sawyer*; Sawyer family, 1962:
Courtesy Grant Sawyer; Richard M. Nixon and Grant Sawyer: *Courtesy
Nevada Historical Society*; Grant Sawyer and John F. Kennedy: *Courtesy
Grant Sawyer*; Grant Sawyer and Lyndon B. Johnson: *Courtesy Grant
Sawyer*.

Cartoons by Ed Kelly. Printed
with permission of the *Las Vegas Review-Journal.*

Hang Tough!

Text and art mechanicals designed by Helen M. Blue.
Camera-ready master composed and printed
at the University of Nevada Oral History Program
in ITC Garamond 1, using WordPerfect 5.2 for Windows
and a Hewlett Packard LaserJet IIISi postscript printer.